THE STORY OF
COINS

by SAM ROSENFELD

Illustrated by
James E. Barry

Checked for Accuracy by Henry Grunthal,
Curator of European and Modern Coins,
The American Numismatic Society

Denarius, drachma, louis d'or, doubloon, shilling, dime—to some these coins represent merely a medium of exchange, but to the coin collector they evoke visions of strange foreign lands and customs, stimulating an interest not only in monetary values but in the geography, history, and even languages of the rest of the world.

An introduction to the exciting and educational hobby of coin collecting, this book tells the fascinating story of coinage, from the beginnings of barter through the development of ancient Greek and Roman civilizations.

A section dealing with the techniques of coin collecting—how to store coins, where to find coins of value, and what kinds of coins to collect—should be of inestimable value to the budding numismatist. Another section, devoted to United States coins, includes a photo story of coin production at the United States Mint and a list of all our commemorative coins.

Profuse illustrations and photographs enable both the beginner and the advanced collector to identify coins and to learn about their place in history.

Although addressed to the young reader, THE STORY OF COINS will prove highly useful to anyone seeking an easy-to-read yet authoritative guide to the popular hobby of coin collecting.

Already well known as the author of *Science Experiments with Water*, *The Magic of Electricity*, and the popular "Ask Me a Question" books, Mr. Rosenfeld has now applied his scientific and storytelling talents to the field of numismatics.

THE STORY OF
COINS

Illustrated by James E. Barry

THE STORY OF
COINS

by SAM ROSENFELD

Checked for Accuracy by Henry Grunthal,
Curator of European and Modern Coins,
The American Numismatic Society

HARVEY HOUSE, INC. · Publishers
Irvington-on-Hudson · New York

A Story of Science Series Book

Acknowledgments

The author is deeply grateful to The American Numismatic Society; to the Money Museum of the Chase Manhattan Bank; to The Coin and Currency Institute, Inc; to Eva Adams, Director of the United States Mint; and to The Whitman Publishing Company, for supplying the photographs appearing in this book, and for their generosity in furnishing advice and answering questions.

HARVEY HOUSE, INC. • Publishers

Irvington-on-Hudson • New York

Contents

To my friends,
Goldie and Hy

1

How Money Began

THOUSANDS OF YEARS AGO man lived a simple life, for most of his needs were only those necessary for his survival. Sometimes, when he hunted for food, he was fortunate and found himself with more food than he could use. Soon, men who liked to hunt began to realize that they could exchange surplus food with someone who preferred to make weapons, fishnets, or clothing. In this way, a man who grew too old to hunt could have food in exchange for the articles he made. This exchange of materials is called "barter." Originally, all trade between people was conducted through barter; and all articles of trade had to be useful as food, clothing, weapons, or implements for hunting.

Man Develops a System of Barter

As man progressed and learned to grow food and to raise cattle, these, too, became items of barter. A man who raised wheat or corn could exchange part of his crop for wool, sheep, cows, or oxen. He might also try to find someone who made plows and was willing to exchange these implements for corn or wheat. In this way, the farmer was able to cultivate his land more efficiently and to increase his wealth. It must be remembered, however, that long ago there was little striving for great wealth, for there was little to spend it on. There were no luxuries, such as television, radio, or automobiles, and there was little or no need for expensive clothing and beautiful furniture. Most people worked where they lived, and the little traveling they did was by means of their own oxen and horses. In this simple way of life, barter served well for hundreds of years and in some areas of the world it still exists.

The Pygmies of Central Africa engage in a type of trade called "dumb barter." It is so called because the individuals exchanging goods do not meet. Thus, there is no discussion about price or quality of goods during a transaction. One tribe leaves its surplus products beneath a tree or hanging from a branch. The next day, other articles, such as corn and fruit, are left in exchange. You, too, may have engaged in barter. Whenever you have traded your baseball cards or books for other cards or books, you have conducted a form of trade that has existed for thousands of years.

As civilization and the population increased, the system of barter began to break down. If land in a certain area was excellent for growing wheat, it might be almost impossible to find a neighbor who would accept wheat in exchange for something else, since he, too, probably grew wheat. The farmer would then have to travel to find a customer or wait for a traveler who might accept his product. As competition increased, this method proved disastrous, since grain could not be stored indefinitely. A new system had to develop.

Cattle as a Medium of Exchange

It was necessary to find a substance that everyone could use and accept, with the idea that if people did not need it at the moment, they could store it and readily exchange it for something else at a later date. This substance is known as a "medium of exchange." Oxen and other cattle were first used for this purpose. Oxen were man's first "machines." They supplied him with the power to till his soil, transport his possessions, pump his water, and grind his wheat into flour. Cattle were so useful

14

that they were used as a medium of exchange even after coins were invented. In early colonial times, cattle were often used to pay taxes. This system became so inconvenient to tax collectors, who also had to argue about the value of the cattle, that during the seventeenth century, laws were passed in many places forbidding the use of cattle or grain in place of money made of metal. The word "capital" arises from the early practice of using cattle as money, for *caput* means "head" in Latin.

As a medium of exchange, cattle were too cumbersome for most people. The cattle often became sick and died, causing great loss of wealth. In addition, cattle had to be fed, which was time-consuming and expensive. It was also difficult to determine a fair exchange between cattle and chickens, grain, cloth, weapons, and farm implements. Another difficulty was that a man had to exchange his entire ox for something of equal value. There was no way to exchange part of an ox for a bag of corn.

Something else, therefore, had to be devised to serve as a convenient medium of exchange. It had to have the following properties:

1. It had to be accepted by almost everyone.

2. It must be divided easily into small parts, so that a trader could exchange part of his wealth for a small item, such as a hoe or a piece of cloth.

3. It had to last a long time, so that people could accumulate it when times were good or when crops were harvested. It could then be spent later.

4. It must be easy to carry.

5. It had to be difficult to imitate, for if it were easily copied, people would lose confidence in it, with a resulting loss in value.

6. It must be easy to count in order to hasten transactions and to determine the exact cost for each person involved.

7. It had to have a certain value, so that it would be accepted by everyone.

8. It had to be easy to recognize.

Early Shell Money

The first form of money may have been shells. Shells were originally used as ornaments. A man with an extra supply of food

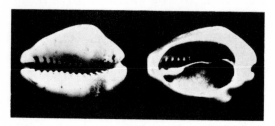

Ancient Chinese Cowrie Shells, About 1000 B.C.

was often willing to exchange some of his food, or anything else he did not want, for a pretty shell that he, or another member of his family, could wear. It became evident that a man with many shells could buy many things. Man began to accumulate wealth by exchanging his labor or the products of his labor, such as clothing, for a certain number of shells. He could then use the shells to buy whatever he wished. The slang expression, "shell out," meaning "to pay up," comes from the original use of shells as money.

Eventually, metals began to be used as money. Metals were convenient to handle, were desirable for use as ornaments, and could be used to make weapons and farm instruments. Since metals were relatively scarce, people could rely on the fact that they would always be valuable; therefore, it was safe to store them for future use. People began to accept metals more and more as a medium of exchange and this medium eventually led to one of man's greatest inventions—coins.

2

Ancient Coins

ALL KINDS OF METALS have been used as money. Iron was used as long ago as 500 B.C. and as recently as 1915 in Germany. In Finland iron coins are still being struck. In 1943, steel was used to make pennies in the United States. At various times, zinc, aluminum, platinum, nickel, bronze, and brass have been used; however, the most popular metals have been gold, silver, and copper.

In 1943 the United States issued a steel cent coated with zinc.

Originally, the metals that were used were in the form of fairly large bars or uneven chunks of metal. As a result, it took a long time to buy anything, for it was necessary to weigh the metal at each transaction in order to determine its value. Since it was inconvenient for a person to carry large chunks of metal, these were later divided into smaller lumps which, however, still had to be weighed. The idea then arose of marking each piece of metal with its weight, in order to save time. The weight was stamped with a wedge-shaped die. These hard metal dies were

17

called "coins." The word "coin" was used to describe the piece of metal that was to be used as money.

The Money of China

Thousands of years ago, cloth, weapons, and farm instruments, such as hoes, spades, chisels, and knives, were used as media of exchange. The use of bronze to fashion these tools originated in the eighteenth century B.C. when it was carried to China by caravans. However, large bronze spades and hoes were difficult to carry, and so trade was hampered.

In 1100 B.C., a wise Chinese ruler ordered that, instead of the real knife or spade, a small metal model of the object itself

Ancient Chinese "Spade Money," About 400 B.C.

could be used. Certain metal coins, now known as "trousers" or "shirt money," were called *pu*. "Knife money" was called *tao*.

Chinese "Pu Money," From Seventh-Fourth Century B.C.

18

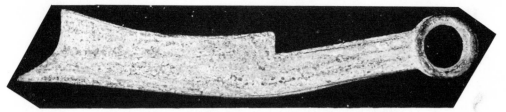

Chinese "Tao," or "Knife Money," From Tenth-Seventh Century, B.C., Actually About Seven Inches Long

Originally, the real knives had a hole in the handle so that they could be hung from a belt. However, they were too heavy and too difficult to handle. The blade of the *tao* was made smaller, until the knives resembled keys. Eventually, only the round top

Chinese "Key Money," A.D. 7-22

of the knife, with its square hole in the center, remained. These were known as "cash" coins.

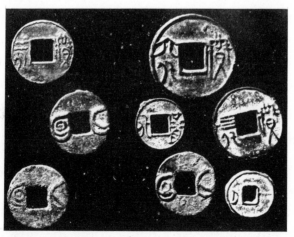

Round Chinese "cash" coins first appeared about the fifth century B.C. and continued until 1919.

The First Western Coins

The first coins to be struck in the world west of China came from Lydia in the seventh century B.C. The ancient Lydians lived in the western part of Asia Minor, at the edge of the Aegean Sea. They used electrum, a mixture of gold and silver found in nature, to mint coins. The rulers of Lydia were very rich, for the country had very fertile soil and abundant natural resources of gold and silver. It was also an important trade center. The Lydians formed pieces of electrum into oval shapes of convenient size and weight and stamped these with official symbols of the state. The obverse

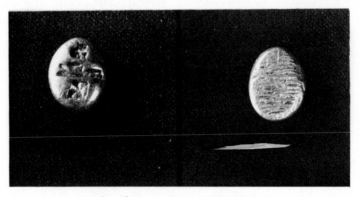

Lydia, Electrum Stater, 700-637 B.C.

side (which shows the main design of a coin) had a picture of a sacred object. The reverse side showed a few sunken parallel lines. These coins were widely used because of their convenience. It was no longer necessary, therefore, to weigh metals at each transaction to determine their value and, since the coins had been issued by the government, their value was assured.

King Croesus and His Coins of Gold

In 560 B.C., Croesus came to the throne of Lydia. His wealth was so great that even now the expression, "rich as Croesus," is used to indicate a wealthy man. King Croesus decided that electrum was unsuitable for producing coins, because its composition as found in nature varied, making it difficult to establish a

Lydia, Gold Stater, 561-546 B.C.

standard value for a particular coin. Since the composition of the metal was difficult to determine, it tempted people to add less expensive metal.

Croesus became the first ruler to use pure gold for minting coins. The obverse side of the coin he made showed the heads of a bull and a lion facing each other. These were the symbols of royal power. The reverse showed a square indentation that was caused by a rectangular punch. In 546 B.C., Croesus lost his throne to the Persians. Only a few specimens of these ancient coins have survived through the centuries to remind us of this once powerful nation.

The Coins of Greece

Ancient Greece was divided into many small cities. Due to the mountainous terrain of Greece, these cities were in little contact with one another, which led them to create independent "city-states" of their own. Some of these city-states are famous to this day—Athens, Sparta, Syracuse, Corinth. Almost all of the city-states of Greece issued coins of their own. The beauty of design and the exquisite workmanship of these coins has not been equaled.

Athens, Silver Dekadrachm, About 480 B.C. Issued to commemorate the Greek victory over the Persians at Marathon in 490 B.C. Obverse: Goddess Athena. Reverse: The Owl of Athens. There is an olive branch at the left of the owl. Compare this coin with the one issued 300 years later.

21

Elis, Silver Stater, 471-452 B.C. Obverse: Eagle with Hare in Its Talons. Reverse: Thunderbolt of Zeus, Ruler of the Gods

The Greeks had an abundance of silver from their silver mines; therefore, most of their coins were made of this metal. The most common unit was called the *stater*. In some sections of Greece, the stater was of gold and was divided into six, twelve, and twenty-four parts. A popular coin, the silver stater of Athens

Rhegium, Silver Tetradrachm, 476-413 B.C. Rhegium was a Greek colony directly across the straits from Sicily. Obverse: Lion's Head. Reverse: Unknown Male Figure

—also called a *tetradrachm*—was worth four *drachmas*. The silver drachma was another popular coin of Greece. It was equal in value to six smaller coins, each of which was called an *obol*.

The earliest coins of Greece were stamped with portraits of gods, goddesses, mythological heroes, or other symbols that identified the city from which each coin came. The reverse had only the punch marks of the die. The punch mark on the reverse was gradually changed to a geometrical design, and this was later changed to a figure of a bull, a temple, a cow, a horse, a battle scene, or a similar figure or event. This custom has remained until the present day.

Abdera, Silver Stater, 390-352 B.C. Abdera was in the southern part of Thrace on the coast of the Black Sea. Obverse: Griffin. In Greek mythology, a griffin was an animal that was half lion and half eagle. Its function was to protect man, guard the earth's treasures, and watch over the dead. Reverse: Head of the Sun God, Apollo, Wearing a Wreath

Aegina

The earliest coins of Greece may have originated on the island of Aegina, which lies about ten miles from the mainland of Greece. This little island could not support its large population, and so many of its people began to trade throughout the Mediterranean. In about 625 B.C., Aegina began to issue silver coins. These were the first pure silver coins ever issued. The obverse had a picture of a sea turtle; the reverse had the mark of the punch that was used to hammer the die into the metal.

Aegina, Silver Stater, 650 B.C. Aegina is a small island in the Aegian Sea, near Athens. Obverse: Sea Turtle with a Line of Dots on Its Shell. Reverse: Sunken (Incuse) Pattern, the Meaning of which Is Unknown Today

These coins are known as "turtles." In about 600 B.C., designs were placed on both sides of the coins.

Aegina continued to issue turtle coins for two hundred years. However, coinage ceased when the island was conquered by Athens. When Aegina regained its freedom, it issued a new series of coins with the picture of a land tortoise to symbolize the loss of sea power.

Aegina, Silver Stater, About 404 B.C. Obverse: Land Turtle (Tortoise), Its Shell Structure Showing Thirteen Plates. Reverse: Divided Square with Letter "A" in One Compartment, a Dolphin in Another, and a Greek Letter in a Third.

Corinth

The city of Corinth, in Greece, was one of the first to mark denominations upon its coins. Until that time, coins were simply recognized as having a certain weight of metal. The amount these would buy at different places depended upon the local value of the metal. By marking the coins with a denomination, a merchant could tell easily how much a coin was worth in Corinth. The symbol that represented Corinth was Pegasus, the mythological winged horse. This figure appeared upon all coins of Corinth, and the coins were called "ponies," or "colts." The reverse sides of these coins were varied to represent different denominations.

Corinth, Silver Stater, About 350 B.C. Obverse: Pegasus, the Mythological Winged Horse. Reverse: Head of Goddess Athena, the Deity of Athens. She is said to have sprung full-grown from the head of her father, Zeus.

Athens

Athens became the most famous of all the cities of Greece. As a result, its currency spread throughout Greece and its colonies, and was readily accepted. Its earliest coins displayed a jar, which was an important product of Athens. This design was abandoned and later issues showed Athena, patron goddess of wisdom, arts, crafts, and defensive warfare; the reverse displayed her owl and her olive branch. These "owls" were issued in several denominations and became the most famous and widely used coins up to the time of Alexander the Great.

Athens, New Style Silver Tetradrachm, 196-88 B.C. Obverse: Head of Goddess Athena, Daughter of Zeus. Reverse: Owl Standing on Amphora, or Wine Jar

Greek coinage spread throughout the ancient world. Nevertheless, local independent states and cities struck their own coins to add to the existing supply, for an inadequate supply of coins made it difficult to transact business. The local coins were usually copies of Greek designs, but they also displayed a picture of the city's favorite god or goddess to identify the origin of the coin. By 400 B.C., so many cities issued coins that confusion arose as to their origin and their value. To overcome this condition, the name of the city-state was placed upon the coins. The finest coins were issued during the fourth and fifth centuries B.C. This fact was particularly true in Sicily and southern Italy, where a large number of beautiful coins were produced.

Leontini, Silver Tetradrachm, 466-422 B.C. Leontini was an inland town of Sicily. Obverse: Apollo Wearing a Laurel Wreath. Reverse: Lion's Head Surrounded by Four Barleycorns

Syracuse

At about this time, Syracuse, in Sicily, was invaded by Carthage. The people of Syracuse repulsed these invasions and, about 480 B.C., they issued a silver *dekadrachm* (ten drachmas) commemorating the victory.

Syracuse, Silver Dekadrachm, About 410 B.C. Obverse: The Head of the Nymph Arethusa, Surrounded by Dolphins. Reverse: The Figure of Nike, Goddess of Victory, Above the Quadriga, or Four-Horse Chariot; Below, a Suit of Armor

About 400 B.C., the Syracusans again repelled the invasions of Carthage. The Athenians also attacked Syracuse, and they, too, were defeated. A large silver dekadrachm was issued to be given as awards to the winners of games and athletic meets that took place in celebration of these victories. This coin is considered to

25

be the most beautiful coin ever issued. The obverse shows the head of Arethusa, a Greek nymph; the reverse shows a man driving a *quadriga*, or four-horse chariot, to which the horses were harnessed abreast.

Macedon

Philip II of Macedon ruled all of Greece between 359 and 336 B.C. He was the first one to establish a uniform coinage that took the place of the many coins that had been minted in the small city-states. Under his reign, the first copper coins appeared.

Macedon, Silver Tetradrachm, 359-336 B.C., Issued by Philip II, Father of Alexander the Great. Obverse: Head of Zeus. Reverse: A Jockey on Horseback, Carrying the Palm Branch of Victory

Alexander the Great, the son of Philip II, came to the throne of Macedon in 336 B.C. He was probably the greatest ruler of ancient times. With a small army of 40,000 men he conquered almost the entire then-known ancient world. As he went from country to country, he ordered the captured mints to melt their coins and to turn out his own coins as a symbol of his authority. Thus, he continued the work of his father by helping to establish a uniform coinage throughout the Greek world.

Most of the coins issued by Alexander the Great were silver tetradrachms, which showed the head of Herakles, the strong man, on one side. On the other side was the figure of Zeus seated upon his throne, with a scepter in one hand and an eagle on the

Macedon, Silver Tetradrachm, 336-323 B.C., Issued by Alexander the Great. Obverse: Head of Herakles, Wearing a Lion's Skin. Reverse: Zeus Seated on His Throne, an Eagle on His Right Hand, in His Left Hand a Scepter. Alexander's name, in Greek letters, is at the right of Zeus.

other. Alexander's name was usually inscribed behind the throne. Herakles, known as Hercules in Roman mythology, was the son of Zeus, king of the gods. Zeus was named Jupiter in Roman mythology. The tetradrachm was the most widely circulated coin of ancient times. It is believed that the head of Herakles is really a portrait of Alexander. This coin continued to be issued for almost two hundred years after Alexander's death.

Thrace, Silver Tetradrachm, 320 B.C., Issued by Lysimachus, King of Thrace. Obverse: Head of Alexander the Great. Note the resemblance to the head of Herakles on the tetradrachm issued by Alexander the Great during his lifetime. Reverse: Goddess Athena Seated

Alexander the Great died of a fever at the age of thirty-three. After his death, several of his generals issued coins with his portrait upon them. Thus, Alexander was the first man to have his

Egypt, Silver Tetradrachm, About 320 B.C., Issued by Ptolemy I. Obverse: Alexander the Great with an Elephant Headdress. Reverse: Goddess Athena

likeness on a coin. In 300 B.C., one of Alexander's generals in Egypt, Ptolemy I, ordered his own portrait to appear on a silver tetradrachm. He became the first living person whose portrait appeared on a coin.

Egypt, Silver Tetradrachm, 323-285 B.C. Obverse: Head of Ptolemy I. Reverse: An Eagle. This design became popular on modern coins.

The Coins of Rome

Livestock served as a medium of exchange for the early Romans until about 350 B.C. The first Roman coins consisted of crude, shapeless lumps of bronze called *aes rude.* Later, about 300 B.C., these were cast into metal bars, or ingots, shaped like flat, thin bricks. They were called *aes signatum,* and were obviously intended to be equal in value to cattle, for both sides often displayed the figure of a bull. The actual value of the metal was

Aes Signatum, About 289 B.C. Bronze Cast in the Form of Flat Rectangular Bars

determined by its weight. Although the bars were inconvenient to handle, their use was a step toward eliminating cattle as a medium of exchange.

Toward the end of the fourth century B.C., the Romans began to issue a cast bronze coin called *aes grave.* One side showed the god Janus, with two faces looking in opposite directions. Janus was the god of all beginnings and was especially worshiped on the first day of each month. January, the first month of the year, is named after him. The other side of the coin displayed the prow of a ship. These coins weighed a pound, but were later reduced

Roman Republic, About 211 B.C. This cast bronze coin has the denomination of one "as." Obverse: Janus, the Two-Headed God of Beginnings and Endings. Reverse: The Prow of a Ship, Symbolizing Roman Sea Power

in weight. As long as the Romans traded among themselves, they were able to use these coins. However, they began to trade with the Greek colonies in southern Italy, whose coins were more beautiful and highly developed. About the third century B.C., in order to compete, the Romans set up a new system of silver coinage. At first, the coins were patterned after Greek models, but later the Romans developed their own characteristic designs.

Roman Republic, Silver Didrachm, About 220 B.C. Obverse: Janus. Reverse: Jupiter Driving a Four-Horse Chariot (Quadriga); Behind Him the Figure of Victory

The most famous of the Roman coins were the silver *denarius* and the bronze *sestertius*, or *sesterce*. It is extremely difficult to compare, with any degree of accuracy, the value of these ancient coins with those of today. Nevertheless, a rough approximation is that a silver denarius was equal to today's United States dollar, and a sesterce was equivalent to its twenty-five cents. One denarius was, therefore, equal to four sesterces. The Romans used images of the gods on one side of their coins; on the reverse, they used figures of victory, heroes, horses, buildings, and important events.

Carthage, Gold Stater, About Fourth Century B.C. Obverse: Head of Tanit, Goddess of Love and Fertility. Reverse: A Horse. Animals were often represented on the coins of Carthage.

In 146 B.C., the Romans destroyed Carthage and completed the conquest of Greece. During the last years of the Roman Republic, their coins began to carry portraits of historic figures, such as Mark Antony, Julius Caesar, Cleopatra, and Brutus. The

Roman Republic, Silver Denarius, 42 B.C. One side: Mark Antony, One of Julius Caesar's Generals. Other side: Octavian, the Grand-Nephew of Julius Caesar, Later His Adopted Son

Roman Republic, Silver Denarius, 43 B.C. Obverse: Brutus. Reverse: Two Daggers, Depicting the Method of Julius Caesar's Assassination. The liberty cap gives the reason; the letters, EID MAR, meaning "Ides of March," give the date. Quite a story on one side of a coin!

 Roman Republic, Silver Denarius, 32-31 B.C. Mark Antony and Cleopatra. Cleopatra, Queen of Egypt, joined Antony in an unsuccessful attempt to overthrow Rome. Their love story ended in disaster for, after their defeat, they both committed suicide.

Roman Empire, Silver Denarius, 27 B.C. Obverse: Caesar Augustus, Known as Octavian Before Becoming the Emperor of Rome. He ruled 27 B.C.-A.D. 14. Reverse: A Crocodile, the Symbol of Egypt, Referring to Its Capture by Augustus

 Roman Empire, Gold Aureus, A.D. 54-68. Obverse: Emperor Nero. He rose to the throne at the age of 17, and is considered to be among the cruelest of all Roman emperors. Reverse: Temple of Vesta, Goddess of Family Piety and the Good Family Life

Roman Empire, Bronze As, A.D. 14-37. Obverse: Emperor Tiberius. Reverse: Globe and rudder, evidence that almost 2000 years ago, people suspected that the earth was round.

 Roman Empire, Brass Dupondius, A.D. 98-117. Obverse: Emperor Trajan. Reverse: A trophy pole on which are hung shields to represent the Conquest of Dacia.

Roman Empire, Bronze Sesterce, A.D. 98-117. Obverse: Emperor Trajan. Reverse: Circus Maximus, a Huge Arena with a Capacity to Seat 260,000 Spectators. Exciting chariot races and athletic events were held here.

coins also bore portraits of their reigning emperors, including Nero, Hadrian, Claudius, Augustus (who was originally known as Octavian), Tiberius, and Trajan. Roman accomplishments and victories were also recorded on their coins. Many of these coins give us a clue to the Roman way of life, for they show pictures of buildings, roads, mints, aqueducts, and bridges. The portrait of the ruling emperor was placed on a coin to help win the loyalty of the many different races and nationalities within the Roman Empire.

Judea, Silver Shekel, A.D. 133-135. Struck During the Second Jewish Revolt, When Hadrian Was Emperor of Rome. Obverse: Temple with the Ark of the Covenant. Reverse: A Bundle of Twigs (Lulav) and a Citron (Esrog)

Judea, Silver Shekel, A.D. 66-70. Struck During the First Jewish Revolt Against Rome. Obverse: A Cup Made of Gold. Reverse: A Branch Bearing Pomegranates

31

Roman Coins Influence Modern Design

The influence of Roman coins upon modern design was even greater than that of Greece. The eagle, which was used by the Greeks and the Romans, is also used on many coins in the United States. The Goddess of Liberty first appeared on Roman coins. The Liberty cap which appears alone, or is worn by the Goddess of Liberty, was worn by Roman slaves to indicate that they

Roman Empire, Bronze As, A.D. 41-54. Obverse: Emperor Claudius. Reverse: Goddess of Liberty Holding a Liberty Cap and Promising Freedom

had been granted their freedom. The design used on United States dimes from 1916-1945 was a *fasces*, a bundle of wooden rods wrapped around an ax and bound together with a thong. This was the symbol of authority of the Roman magistrates. The Romans introduced the practice of placing inscriptions that followed the circular edge of the coin. They also introduced the mint mark (as we know it today) on a coin to identify the place where it had been made.

Roman Empire, Silver Denarius, About 44 B.C. Obverse: Julius Caesar. This is the first Roman coin to portray a living person. Reverse: Sacrificial Implements

Much of the English language is derived from Latin, the language used by the Romans. Of particular interest to the coin collector are the many Latin words encountered in our study of coins. The motto that appears on the United States coins, E PLURIBUS UNUM, is a Latin phrase that means "many joined into one." The words, "quarter, dime, cent, and coin," are derived from Latin. Numismatics, the science of coins, comes from the Latin expression, *numisma*, which means "coin." The words,

Roman Empire, Gold Aureus, A.D. 54. Obverse: Head of Emperor Nero and His Mother Agrippina. Reverse: EX SC Within a Wreath. The letters stood for ex senatus consulto, *by decree of the Senate.*

Roman Empire, Gold Aureus, A.D. 37. Obverse: Emperor Caligula. Reverse: A Deified Emperor (Possibly Augustus) Wearing a Crown

"obverse," "reverse," and "debt" are but a few more examples of words we owe to Latin.

Because of their age, it may appear to be costly to build a collection of Greek and Roman coins. Actually, the opposite is true. Some interesting bronze coins can be purchased for as little as a dollar! Silver and gold coins, naturally, are more expensive.

The reason so many of these ancient coins are inexpensive is that the Greek and Roman states existed for many years and issued thousands of different types of coins in the numerous city-states and over the vast Roman Empire. Coins are being dug up constantly throughout Europe, Asia, and Africa by archeologists digging into ruins and by farmers tilling their soil. There being no banks, people used to bury their wealth in the ground. Some of these people died, others were taken into slavery, thus leaving their coins undiscovered beneath the earth. If you are fortunate enough to own one of these ancient coins, can you help wondering through whose hands it passed two thousand years ago? Was it a soldier who buried his small wealth before going into battle, and who never returned? Was it owned by a king? Or did it belong to a family—perhaps one much like your own? For a moment, the past becomes real, as you can almost sense someone long ago handling the same coin you now hold in your hand.

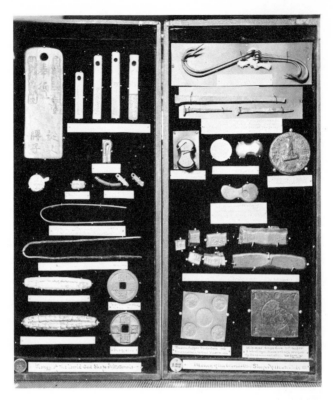

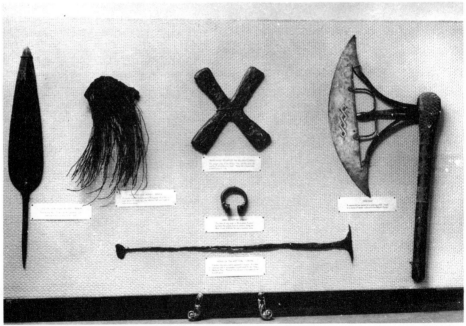

Exhibits in the Chase Money Museum of the Chase Manhattan Bank in New York City

34

3

Odd Money—Past and Present

MANY STRANGE DEVICES have been used in the past, and many are still in use, to serve man's need for money with which to trade and barter. Possibly the oldest form of money was the seashell. The cowrie shell was used in China for many centuries and is still used in many islands of the Pacific and in parts of Africa. These shells were useful as ornaments or as charms to drive away evil spirits. The North American Indians used shell money called wampum.

Stone Money of Yap

One of the strangest forms of currency originated in the Pacific island of Yap, about 500 miles southwest of Guam. These "coins" consisted of huge stone disks that looked like millstones. They were called *fe* or *fei*, and ranged in size from several inches

Stone Money of Yap. A Yap "coin" about 30 inches in diameter weighs over 100 pounds and is equal in value to 10,000 coconuts, one quarter acre of land, or a wife.

35

in diameter to great, flat stones ten to twelve feet across. The stones had a hole through the middle so that they could be carried on poles. The stones from which these coins were made came from quarries on the Pelew Islands about 400 miles away, or from Guam or neighboring islands.

The value of these coins was derived from the labor and the danger involved in obtaining the stones from the quarries. These massive objects had to be transported by raft for hundreds of miles. Many of the rafts never returned. In addition, it was expensive to quarry on neighboring islands, for the local island chiefs had to be given food and gifts in exchange for permission to work the quarries. The smaller stones bought small items, such as fish and vegetables. When small change was required, shell money was used. Today, these stones are no longer used as money; they remain propped against huts and trees and are used during village ceremonies.

Strange Forms of Money

In many places throughout the world, teeth, at one time, were used as money. In the Solomon and Bismarck Islands, the

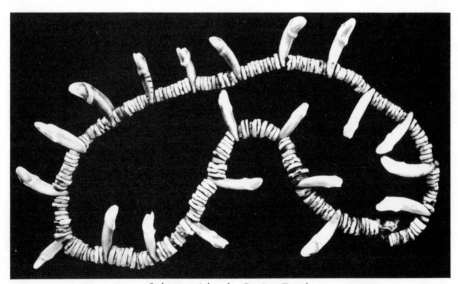
Solomon Islands, Canine Teeth

Alaska, Tooth Money Used by Whalers

teeth of wild dogs were strung together. In the Fiji Islands, whale teeth and the jawbones of fruit-eating bats were used as money. In many of the South Sea Islands, the teeth of porpoises, whales, and fish were valuable.

There are many other odd forms of money. In Portuguese West Africa, elephant-tail bristles were a favorite currency. Woodpecker scalps were used by the Indians of Oregon and California, and in southern California clam disks were used as

Portuguese West Africa, Elephant Tail Bristles

money. In places as widely separated as Alaska and Ceylon, fish-hooks were used as a medium of exchange.

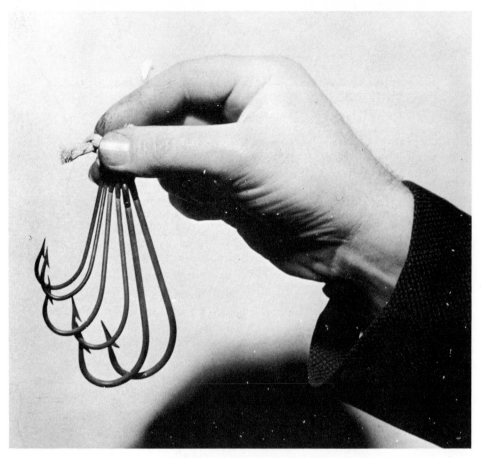

Alaskan Fishhook Money

In some parts of Mexico, the natives used soap as money. The Aztec Indians of Mexico used cocoa beans. The beans were often stored in sacks containing almost 25,000 beans. The Aztecs also circulated quills filled with gold dust, as well as flat pieces of copper hoe money.

At one time, porcelain was a legal medium of exchange in China. Also, in China, salt and tea were used as money. Each of these items was pressed into bricks which were actually stamped by the government to attest to the value. The tea was often mixed

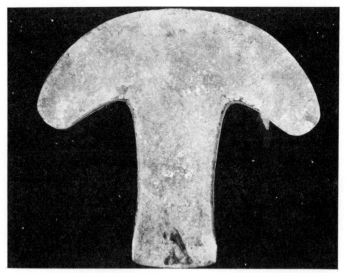

Mexican Hoe Money, Used as a Medium of Exchange for Many Centuries. It may also have served as a potter's tool.

with sawdust to keep it from falling apart. Tea is sometimes used as money to this day on trade routes between China and Tibet.

Russian Tea Money

Salt Money

Salt has been a fairly common medium of exchange because of its value in flavoring and preserving food. The Roman soldiers were paid in salt so often that the word "salary" comes from the Latin word, *salarium*, money given to soldiers for purchase of salt. Today we say that a good worker is "worth his salt."

In the African Congo, many of the people who work on roads are paid in buckets of salt because of its scarcity and the necessity to flavor the vegetable diet. It is also necessary, for health

West Africa, Salt Money from Sierra Leone. This container weighs four pounds. Anyone interested in purchasing a wife must offer twelve of these containers.

reasons, to replace the body salt that is lost through perspiration while working in tropical climates.

In Ethiopia, cloth, salt, and glass beads of various shapes and colors were used as currency. Near the Baltic Sea, amber served as money because of its usefulness as an ornament and as a good-luck charm. Amber is a fossil resin that oozed out of a tree that has been extinct for centuries. An unusual use for money is encountered in the Belgian Congo, where flat copper crosses are used to purchase wives.

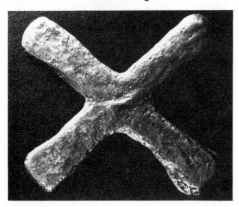

Congo, Copper Cross from the Baluba Tribe of Katanga. One of these crosses would purchase about twenty pounds of flour; one hundred crosses, a wife.

In many areas of the world, food was used as money. The Bible mentions grain as a medium of exchange. It was widely used as money thousands of years ago and is still being used in parts of China, India, and Mexico. The kind of food used for money varied with what the people ate or could produce.

Metal money of all kinds has been used. Iron, copper, gold, and silver, in the form of lumps, bricks, rings, axes, pots, bells, shoes, weapons, and tools have all been used as money. In Liberia

Egypt, Gold Ring Money, About 1000 B.C.

and Sierra Leone, thin iron rods, twelve to eighteen inches long, are used. These are called *Kissi pennies*, and are named after the tribe that uses them.

The needle money of southern Nigeria consists of thin needles only one half inch long. Several thousand of these could purchase a slave. In parts of New Guinea, boar tusks were valuable. The feathers of a small bird could buy a wife in the Santa Cruz Islands, and the natives of Easter Island accepted dead rats.

The people of Malacca, on the Malay Archipelago, had an unusual form of money made of tin and shaped like a tree. The coins were cast on a trunk in the form of branches. When a

Malaccan wanted to purchase something, he simply broke off as many of the coins as he needed.

Malayan Money Tree

A Wooden Nickel Used as Money During Difficult Economic Times in the United States

In the United States, wooden nickels, notes made of sheepskin or buckskin, nails, tobacco, furs, and blankets were used as money at various times in history. In 1685, the French in Canada used playing cards as money! The governor wrote an amount on the face of a playing card and signed his name. These cards were used to pay the soldiers. This form was not too different from our own dollar bills which simply state that they are backed by a certain amount of silver. The latest United States dollars do not even mention silver. They are simply worth ONE DOLLAR.

This clearly illustrates that if a government is strong and has the confidence of the people, *anything* can be used as money.

4

How Money Is Coined

A COIN IS basically a metal disk with an image stamped upon it on one or both sides.

Ancient Minting Methods

In ancient times, the metal was hammered to the desired thickness, and the edges were shaped with a sharp instrument. Since this work had to be done for each coin, the process took a long time, and no two coins were exactly alike. Also, the expense of making each coin would have been very high were it not for the fact that much of the work was done by slaves.

In order to produce an image upon a piece of metal, the metal was placed upon a die. This die was made of hardened bronze or iron which had engraved upon it the image that was to be hammered into the coin. The image had been engraved into the die by hand by highly skilled craftsmen. The die was pointed at one end so that it could be set in a hole carved out of a block of wood or an anvil. A silver or a gold disk was heated so that it would be softened, and a workman, using a pair of tongs, placed it on the die. This die, called the obverse, contained the main design, such as the head of a monarch or a god. Another die, which was to be used as a punch, was set on top of the metal disk. This die, known as the reverse, was sharply struck with a hammer, impressing an image upon the coin. At first, the simple marks of the punch were on the reverse of the coin. Later, an image was engraved on the punch so that both sides of the coin contained a design.

The thickness of the coins and the depth of the impressions varied slightly from coin to coin, since it was not possible for all workmen to use exactly the same force to hammer out an image. In addition, the temperature of the metal varied slightly for different coins. Sometimes the punch would move after the first blow, and a double impression would appear on the coin.

At a later stage in the development, an image was engraved directly upon a pair of tongs. The blank metal disk was placed between the dies of the tongs, and the dies were struck by a hammer. In this way, there was a greater chance that the design would be impressed more evenly.

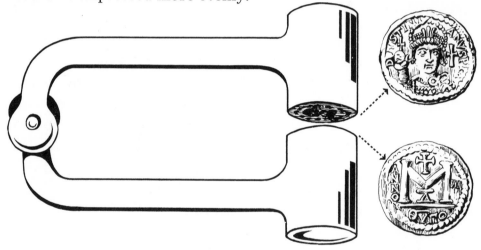

An ancient coining press used by the Roman Emperor Constans, who reigned A.D. 337-350.

Modern Minting Methods

United States coins are manufactured by the Bureau of the Mint, which is part of the Treasury Department. From 1962 to 1965, there were two coinage mints in operation, one located in Denver and the other in Philadelphia. On September 1, 1965, under the Coinage Act of 1965, minting operations were resumed at the San Francisco Assay Office. The one-cent and five-cent

United States Mint, Philadelphia, Pennsylvania

United States Mint, Denver, Colorado

pieces, which were dated 1965, were the first coins to be produced at that Office since 1955.

Until the Coinage Act, the composition of the silver dollar, half dollar, quarter dollar, and dime consisted of a mixture containing 90 percent silver and 10 percent copper. However, no silver dollars have been coined since 1935. The so-called "minor" coins are five-cent pieces and one-cent pieces. The five-cent coins

United States Mint, San Francisco, California

are composed of 75 percent copper and 25 percent nickel. The cents are of bronze and contain 95 percent copper and 5 percent zinc.

The Coinage Act, passed July 23, 1965, changed the composition of the dime, the quarter, and the half dollar. All silver was eliminated from the dime and the quarter; the silver in the half

47

dollar was reduced from 90 percent to 40 percent. The cent and the nickel were not changed by the new legislation.

The dime and the quarter are manufactured from strips composed of three layers of metal bonded together and rolled to the required thickness. This process is called "cladding." The faces of the coins are 75 percent copper and 25 percent nickel, which is the same as the copper-nickel alloy used in the current five-cent piece. The inside of the "sandwich" is pure copper, which can be seen at the edges of the coins. The new fifty-cent piece consists of outer layers that are 80 percent silver and 20 percent copper. The core consists of 21 percent silver and 79 percent copper. This proportion gives the entire coin an overall composition of 40 percent silver.

Early coin presses were operated by hand. Today's high-speed coin presses, electrically operated, are capable of producing over seven thousand coins per hour. (United States Mint, Philadelphia)

Coinage Operations

Modern coins are struck by machines that are capable of producing up to 130 coins per minute. The pure metals are weighed accurately in amounts necessary to produce the correct proportions for a particular coin. In order to combine these metals in a mixture called an "alloy," the metals are melted in electric furnaces.

It is possible to follow the various steps in the production of nickels and pennies by means of photographs of coinage operations at the United States Mint in Philadelphia. The preparation of the metal strip needed to make the new half dollars, quarters, and dimes does not take place at the Mint. It is prepared commercially and arrives at the Mint ready for stamping as described in step 5.

Step 1—The metal is melted in an electric furnace. At the top is a view of the furnace, from which molten metal is poured into the water-cooled mold which casts the coinage ingots in the form of long, fairly thin bars.

Step 1   Step 2

Step 2—The ingots are in a storage cradle, ready to be sent through rollers that will squeeze them to the proper size.

Step 3—The ingots are passed through rolling mills several times in order to reduce them to long strips of the exact thickness required for the coin being produced. This is the first reducing operation on what is called the "No. 1 breakdown mill."

Step 4—This is the final rolling operation in the finish mill. Here the strip is reduced to the desired size.

Step 3

Step 4

Step 5—The new coin takes its shape in this high-speed punch press. The strip is fed in at the right. Blank coins, called "planchets," are punched from the strip and are ejected into the "tote" box on the left.

Step 6—In the process of rolling and punching, the metal becomes hard and must be softened by heating. This process is called "annealing." In this annealing furnace, the blanks are softened, then cleaned and dried.

Step 7—Machines sometimes make mistakes in stamping. The machine in this step is known as a "riddling machine," where imperfect blanks are separated from perfect blanks.

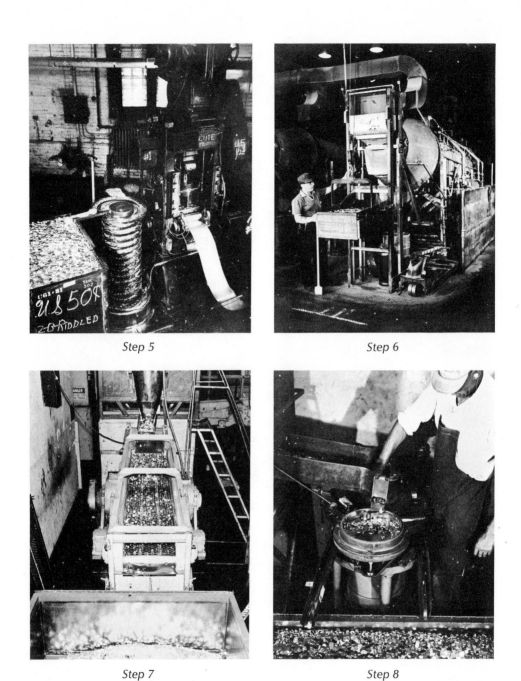

Step 5

Step 6

Step 7

Step 8

Step 8—The blanks are fed into this milling, or "upsetting," machine which produces a raised, or "upset," rim. This rim gives the coins a longer life by protecting them against abrasion.

Step 9

Step 9—The planchets go through a coin press where, in a single stroke, the dies stamp designs on the obverse and the reverse. The stamped coins shown in the photograph are being inspected for possible defects.

Step 10

Step 10—The finished coins are counted, placed in a bag, and weighed. The filled bags are sewn at the top by a sewing machine. Dimes, quarters, and half dollars are each sacked at one thousand dollars per bag; nickels are sacked two hundred dollars per bag; pennies are sacked fifty dollars per bag. The coins are then sent to Federal Reserve Banks.

52

5

How to Start a Coin Collection

COIN COLLECTING is one of the oldest and most popular of hobbies. This pastime fascinated the ancient Greeks and Romans, who collected their own coins and the coins of other nations. The Popes of the thirteenth and fourteenth centuries and many Italian noblemen enjoyed coin collecting during the Renaissance period that extended from the fourteenth to the sixteenth centuries. There were also many coin enthusiasts in England during the sixteenth and seventeenth centuries.

As you can see, the coin collector has had good company in the past, and he continues in good company in the present. Interest in coin collecting has spread throughout the world. People in all walks of life—lawyers, doctors, elevator operators, postmen, college professors, and boys and girls on farms and in cities have been attracted to this fine hobby.

Why has this interest in coin collecting persisted, and why has it spread so rapidly in the past few years? Coins have always created interest because of the history and the stories they tell about a country. It is interesting to read about ancient Rome, and then to have the story come alive by looking at a coin and seeing an actual portrait of a Roman emperor or the picture of a building that no longer exists. It is a thrill to realize that the coin was struck so many hundreds and hundreds of years ago, and has been able to outlast so many civilizations. Thousands of years from today, people may look at coins, such as the United States

Franklin half dollar, and wonder at the story of that great American inventor and statesman.

Another reason for the spectacular increase in coin collecting is that the value of coins has risen rapidly in the past few years. A collector who studies coins and purchases wisely has many opportunities for profit. Also, since leisure time is increasing for a large segment of the American population, a collector can spend many happy hours arranging and studying his collection. He also has the opportunity to meet people and make friends at coin clubs and at the coin shows that are now being held so frequently in many cities in the United States.

But how does a coin collector get started? The simplest way is to begin with the coins you already have. Examine several pennies. (It should, perhaps, be pointed out at this time that there is disagreement among coin collectors as to the use of the word "pennies." Some insist that these are "cents.") You may be surprised to see something you may have never noticed before. The portrait of Abraham Lincoln appears on all of these coins, but some pennies have two stalks of wheat on the reverse; whereas others have a picture of a building. What is the building, and when did the change in design take place? Those of you who are curious to know the answer to this question, will be interested in learning that it is the Lincoln Memorial in Washington, D.C. It was introduced on the Lincoln cent in 1959, which was the

What is the name of the building shown on this coin?

150th anniversary of Lincoln's birthday. Perhaps you may wish to compare the fine image on the coin with the actual building in Washington. Many collectors have made such trips to all parts of the world after seeing certain monuments, rivers, or buildings on their coins. The process of searching for information and finding the answers is so satisfying that it will cause you to become more and more interested in your collection. You will want to see it grow, and you will become more excited as you approach your goal of completing a certain series of coins.

Every word and every image on a United States coin has a story behind it. There are coins showing frontiersmen, Indians, the California Gold Rush, statesmen, presidents, ships, maps, and many other interesting aspects of a nation. The beginning collector soon realizes that the best way to make a collection grow is to specialize in certain types of coins.

Which Coins Should You Collect?

There is no strict rule for specialization. You will make your own decisions as you learn more about coins and begin to prefer some coins over others. Some people like to collect all the coins of a single type, that is, all Roosevelt dimes from the date of issue to the present day. This is a good coin with which to begin,

Roosevelt Dimes, Issued in 1946

since these coins are relatively easy to obtain and will encourage the beginner to expand his collection. You may prefer to collect Indian Head coins, or the large cents that were issued at certain periods in the development of our country. Some collectors specialize in commemorative coins that are issued to celebrate certain historical events. Others have "ship" collections, or bird, church, animal, and even hat collections. You may decide to collect coins by the year, and to obtain as many coins as possible

"Animal" Coin Collection

of each year in a certain period of our history. Or you may prefer ancient coins or coins of another country. In coin collecting, you will make your own rules and change these to give you the most enjoyment.

Where can you find interesting coins?

1.   Go through your pockets each day and select the coins you need for your collection.

2.   Tell your friends about your hobby. Often they, too, will become interested in your search and will look for coins if you give them a list. Sometimes a friend or a relative may have a valuable coin that he has been saving for years, and which he might be willing to give to you because of your interest.

3.   When you buy any article, do not give the storekeeper or clerk the exact amount, so that you may receive change.

4.   Purchase a coin catalogue and note the prices of coins. You will learn the value of coins, and so be in a better position to judge a wise purchase when the opportunity comes.

5. Make a list of the coins that you need to fill your collection and also note their value.

6. Join a local coin club—there's nothing that gives a collector more satisfaction than to share his stories about coins with another collector, or to boast about his coin collection. It also gives collectors an opportunity to swap or purchase coins from one another.

7. Subscribe to a coin magazine or newspaper to learn about the latest finds, stories, and prices.

You may purchase special United States Mint sets struck for coin collectors at the San Francisco Assay Office. The sets include one specimen of a cent, a nickel, a dime, a quarter, and a half dollar. These are priced at $5.00 a set. The coins are struck one at a time and have a more brilliant surface and a higher relief than regular coins. To order these Mint sets, your check or money order should be made out to: Officer in Charge, U.S. Assay Office, and addressed to: U.S. Assay Office, Numismatic Service, 350 Duboce Avenue, San Francisco, California 94102.

What Determines the Value of a Coin?

It is wise to learn what makes a coin valuable. The main factors are the rarity of the coin, the demand for the coin, and the condition of the coin. Condition is so important that a coin in poor condition may sell for fifty cents; whereas the same type of coin in excellent condition may cost ten to one hundred times as much. If, at any time, you have the choice between buying two or three coins in poor condition, or buying one coin in fine condition, it is almost always wiser to buy the finer coin. Your collection will be respected more by others, and the coin will be much easier to sell at a later date. What is equally important is that a coin in fine condition goes up in value more rapidly than a poor one, because of the greater scarcity and greater demand.

In order to determine the value of a coin according to its condition, coin experts have established the following classification:

Proof (Pr.): This type of coin has a mirror-like surface and is struck primarily for collectors. It is made with a specially polished die and a polished blank; it is sold by mints at a premium.

Uncirculated (Unc.): A new coin, which finds its way, immediately after release, into the hands of a collector. Uncirculated coins show no signs of wear or damage. They have a brilliant luster, but may show some tarnish as they get older.

Extremely Fine (Ex. F. or XF): This coin has been circulated slightly. The highest points of the design show only the slightest amount of wear.

Very Fine (V.F.): The high spots on this coin show definite signs of wear, but the design and the letters are sharp and easily discernible.

Fine (F.): The high spots on the coin are definitely worn. The coin has obviously been circulated, but the basic design is still clear.

Very Good (V.G.): Shows a good deal of wear, but the lettering is clear. There may be scratches, but there are no serious gouges or blemishes.

Good (G.): Minimum conditions that a coin collector will accept. The letters are still readable, and most of the design is distinguishable.

Fair (Fr.): These coins are usually not sought by collectors. The letters and much of the design show a great deal of wear, although the coin is easily identified.

Mints and Mint Marks

One of the chief guides to the investment value of a coin is the mint mark. A mint mark is a small letter placed on a coin to show where it was struck. A description of the location of mint

Lincoln Cent, D Mint Mark

marks is given in Chapter 12. This practice was introduced by the Romans. The following is a list of United States mints, past and present:

MINT LOCATION	YEARS	MINT MARK
Philadelphia, Pa.	1792 to present	none (except P, 1942-1945)
Dahlonega, Ga.	1838-1861	D
Charlotte, N.C.	1838-1861	(gold coins only) C
New Orleans, La.	1838-1909	(gold coins only) O
San Francisco, Calif.	1845-1955; 1965 to present	S
Carson City, Nev.	1870-1893	CC
Denver, Colo.	1960 to present	D

Coins issued at the Philadelphia Mint have no mint mark. The exception to this rule is the Jefferson nickel that did have a small P to indicate its origin. The coin was issued during the war years of 1942-1945, and was a five-cent piece rather than a "nickel," for it contained only the metals copper, silver, and manganese. Nickel was not used because it was a vital war material and was in short supply.

Jefferson Five-Cent Piece, P Mint Mark

Since some mints struck fewer coins than others, the mint mark is important in determining the scarcity of a coin and, as we have seen, coins that are scarce are usually more valuable. However, this is not always true, for some coins have become valuable despite a large issue. Nevertheless, the usual rule is

Liberty Seated Half Dollar. Reverse: CC Mint Mark

Indian Head Gold Dollar. Reverse: D Mint Mark

Liberty Seated Half Dollar. Reverse: S Mint Mark

"O" Mint Mark on Reverse of Liberty Seated Half Dime

that where a coin has been struck by more than one mint, the coin issued in smaller quantities is priced higher. One example of this is the 1920 Indian Head (Buffalo) nickel that was issued at three mints. A 1920-S or 1920-D nickel is worth seven or eight times as much as a 1920 nickel struck at the Philadelphia mint. Compare the number of coins struck at each mint:

	QUANTITY ISSUED
1920	63,093,000
1920-S	9,689,000
1920-D	9,418,000

Clear plastic tubes hold rolls of coins of varying denominations.

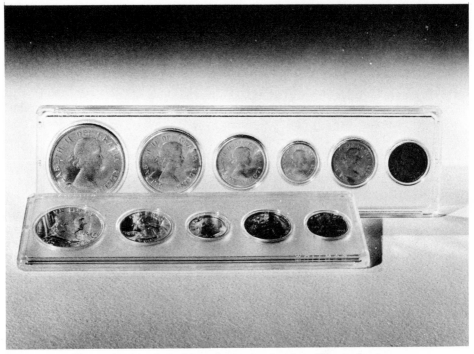

These plastic coin holders display both sides of a set of coins.

6

How to Take Care of Coins

A SERIOUS COIN COLLECTOR guards his collection carefully, for he knows that the beauty and the value of his collection will increase with time only if his coins are in good condition. Though metal may seem hard and durable, coins are easily scratched and marred by improper handling.

If a coin must be handled, it should be picked up by its edges, never at the center, for the perspiration that makes fingerprints can cause a coin to become discolored. Also, do not place more than one coin in an envelope or a bag, for the coins will collide with one another, causing scratches. This is particularly true for heavier coins, such as half dollars and dollars. Needless

to say, dropping coins or tapping them to hear their sound does the coins no good. It is also unwise to use rubber bands to keep coins together, or to wrap them in paper, for these materials contain substances, such as sulfur, which will tarnish the metal.

Some collectors put lacquer on their coins to protect them from the oxygen and the sulfur compounds in the air. However, there is a risk in doing so, for this makes it more difficult to dispose of the coin later. Many collectors like their coins "pure," and the slightest amount of foreign material, even lacquer, will cause them to lose interest in a coin.

How to Clean Coins

Most collectors prefer to purchase coins that have not been cleaned. For some collectors, an old coin that has been cleaned is actually undesirable, because it has lost the "mark of time" that often makes a coin appear more beautiful.

Cleaning a coin, even a recent coin, does not make it more valuable. A coin in the "Good" category cannot be brought to the "Very Good" classification by making it shiny. An experienced collector carefully examines the details and the lettering on a coin to determine its condition. No amount of cleaning can restore letters or designs that have been worn away. Actually, it may do the opposite; besides bringing out scratches and gouges more clearly, the very act of removing tarnish carries away some of the material that makes up the coin, and an otherwise acceptable coin may be ruined. Nevertheless, many collectors feel that they are going to keep their collection indefinitely, and they like to see them as bright as possible.

A silver coin will tarnish if it is not handled fairly frequently. Handling keeps it "silvery," because the tarnish that is slowly formed upon exposure to the air is rubbed off by the fingers. Unfortunately, a small amount of the coin is lost in the process. If you wish to clean your silver coins, make a paste of baking soda (not baking powder) and water. Rub the coin gently with a soft cloth and wash off the paste under warm, running water. Dry it with a soft flannel cloth or a facial tissue. This process may also be used to clean nickel coins. You can also clean silver or copper coins with household ammonia mixed with water to make a weak solution. The surface grime on copper and bronze coins can often be removed by rubbing gently with olive oil soaked in a soft cloth. A word of caution: Do not use a metal scouring pad, scouring powder, wire brush, eraser, or metal polish to clean a coin. If you intend to clean coins it is best to practice on those that you do not expect to keep for your collection.

How to Store Coins

Coins are stored in order to protect them from scratches, handling, and the action of the air. They may be stored so as to display them as an exhibit that can be seen and enjoyed, or they may be put safely away for months or years in the hope that their value will increase.

One of the most popular methods of storing coins is to place them in coin albums and coin boards. These have been designed to hold all types of United States and foreign coins. The coins

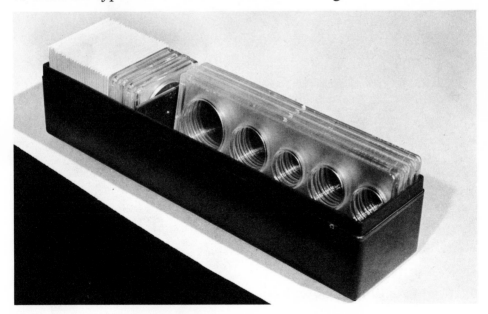

are pressed into individual holes in the board, where they are held tightly in place and can be seen from both sides. As an added convenience to the coin collector, each one of these boards has three holes punched along the margin so that it can be placed in a specially designed three-ring binder. In this way, the collector can reserve one whole binder for nickels, another for pennies or dimes; or he can mix pages of coins to suit his own purposes. The date, the mint mark, and the number of coins issued are printed below each coin opening.

Other types of albums are designed for individual series of coins, such as Lincoln cents or Buffalo nickels. These are bound like books and are easy to display. The coins fit into holes and are protected between two sliding panels of clear plastic. Included in these albums is information that is helpful to collectors. Each volume of coins also contains mint marks, the quantity of coins minted, and a brief background history of the coins. Most of these albums and coin boards are inexpensive, and they provide the collector with an excellent means of storing coins systematically in a compact space.

 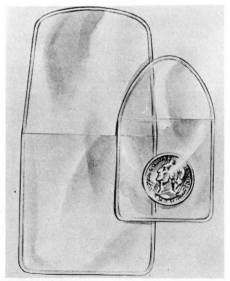

Different Types of Coin Holders for Displaying Individual Coins

Sometimes a collector may wish to mount a coin separately, either because it is his favorite, or because he may wish to carry it. Individual holders of clear lucite plastic have been designed for this purpose. Clear plastic envelopes, or tarnish-free paper for individual coins, and clear plastic tubes to hold stacks of coins by denomination, are also available.

These book-type coin albums display coins on both sides and, at the same time, protect them from scratches and handling.

7

The Beginning of American Coins

IN THE DAYS before the white man settled in North America, life for the Indians was simple. As with any people who depend mainly on their natural habitat for survival, there was no real need for money. If a man wanted food for his family and himself, he would fish or hunt. His wife would cook, sew, and, perhaps, farm. If a family needed a home, they built it out of the skins of animals and used poles made out of trees. If they wanted to travel, they made canoes by hollowing out the trunks of trees. However, there was some use for money among the Indians, for there was always the possibility of trading for a better canoe, for pelts, horses, or arrows. The Indian medium of exchange was known as wampum. This form of money was made from sea-shells, which were strung together like beads. The Indians polished each shell laboriously and made a hole in it with a sharp stone.

The shells came in two colors—black (or dark purple) and white. The black shells or beads were twice as valuable as the white beads. In addition to their use as money, wampum was also used for ornamental purposes. Wampum beads were also woven into belts and used as symbols of war and peace among some Indian tribes.

The English and the Dutch colonists accepted wampum as money, and actually placed a value upon it by law. For instance,

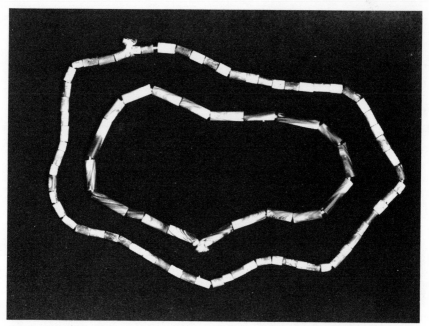

Wampum was used in payment of tributes, as gifts, or in the purchase of a wife.

in 1643, a string of eight white beads was valued at one penny; four black beads had the same value.

On the west coast of America, Indians used a different kind of shell money called *dentalium* (plural: *dentalia*). These shells were about an inch long and looked like small walrus tusks. Three hundred sixty of these beads strung upon caribou sinew were called a "fathom," known among the Indians as *allikochik*, or "human beings their shell money."

An Early Example of Inflation

Shell money became so popular that the colonists set up factories in New England, New York, and Virginia to make these beads. The use of faster and better methods of polishing the shells and the use of metal drills to make holes enabled the colonists to manufacture such a vast number of shells that they eventually lost their value as money. This undue expansion or increase of shells ("currency") probably constituted one of the earliest examples of inflation in the United States. The value of wampum as money had been established because of the labor involved in finding shells, polishing them, boring holes carefully, and stringing them. The use of wampum as money ended about the year 1720, and tobacco and liquor became popular as the media of exchange. Subsequently, however, laws were passed in the Colonies making it illegal to use liquor as money.

Other forms of money in the Colonies were musket balls and gunpowder, both of which were valuable because they were necessary for hunting and for self-protection. Nails were also a medium of exchange for they were important in building houses and making farm implements.

Hand-Wrought Nails Used as Money in Colonial New England. Originally, "pennynail" was used to designate the size and cost of nails per hundred; it now denotes their length, beginning at one inch for twopenny nails and increasing, by quarter inches, up to tenpenny.

Soon the British passed laws forbidding the colonists to make their own nails or to sell tobacco and other products to one another. Instead, the colonists had to sell many of their products to England, and the English traders would then sell these back to other colonists. This raised the prices so much and caused such a flow of money out of the Colonies, that the people were always short of money to carry on business transactions. The colonists asked the British Treasury to supply them with coins, but their requests were ignored. To make matters worse, England forbade the colonists to coin their own money—one of the issues that led to the American Revolution.

Coins of Many Nations

There was some metal money in the Colonies at this time, but these coins came from foreign lands. The first coinage issued for the colonists, in about 1616, came from Bermuda, then known as the Sommer Islands. These coins, which were made of copper or brass and lightly silvered, were called "Hog Money."

Sommer Islands, Hog Money, About 1616

They received this name because they had a picture of a hog on one side; the other side showed a four-masted ship.

Many other foreign coins circulated among the Colonies. There were English pence, shillings, pounds, and guineas. There were also the French *louis d'or*, the Italian *sequin*, the German *taler*, and a number of Spanish coins, such as the gold *doubloon* and silver *peso*.

The peso, or Spanish milled dollar, was the forerunner of our modern silver dollar. It was the most popular coin of the American colonies, and was known as the "pillar dollar," or "piece of eight." It was made famous in pirate fiction, particularly in Robert Louis Stevenson's *Treasure Island*, wherein a parrot keeps shouting, "Pieces of eight! Pieces of eight!" The coin was called a "piece of eight" because it was worth eight Spanish *reales* (royals). Since this was a large unit of money, it was often broken into two, four, or eight parts. The smaller parts were called "bits," and each bit was worth twelve and one-half cents. Therefore, "two bits" was a quarter of a dollar; a half dollar was four bits—expressions still in use today.

The Spanish pieces of eight were originally struck in Spain, but were later struck in Mexico. These coins were so popular

72

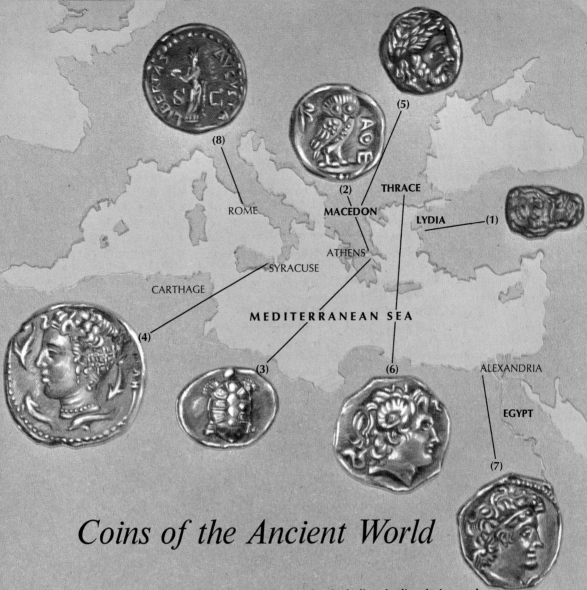

Coins of the Ancient World

(1) Lydia, Gold Stater, 561-546 B.C., showing the heads of a bull and a lion facing each other.

(2) Athens, Silver Dekadrachm, about 480 B.C., issued to commemorate the Greek victory over the Persians at Marathon in 490 B.C. The coin shows the Owl of Athens.

(3) Aegina, Silver Stater, about 404 B.C. A land turtle (tortoise), its shell structure showing thirteen plates.

(4) Syracuse, Silver Dekadrachm, about 410 B.C., showing the head of the nymph Arethusa, surrounded by dolphins.

(5) Macedon, Silver Tetradrachm, 359-336 B.C., issued by Philip II, father of Alexander the Great, showing the head of Zeus.

(6) Thrace, Silver Tetradrachm, 320 B.C., issued by Lysimachus, King of Thrace, showing head of Alexander the Great.

(7) Egypt, Silver Tetradrachm, 323-285 B.C., showing head of Ptolemy I.

(8) Roman Empire, Bronze As, A.D. 41-54. Goddess of Liberty holding a liberty cap and promising freedom.

The first coins west of China came from Lydia in the seventh century B.C. In 560 B.C., King Croesus of Lydia became the first ruler to make coins of pure gold. The Greeks continued to design coins of great beauty and initiated many customs in design which have remained until the pesent day. The earliest coins of Greece were stamped with mythological figures or symbols that identified the city in which each coin originated. Alexander the Great was the first human being whose likeness appeared on a coin.

The influence of Roman coins upon modern design was even greater than that of Greece. The eagle, which was used by the Greeks and

the Romans, appears on many United States coins. The Romans also introduced the mint mark on a coin to identify the place where it had been made. As nations fell and new nations arose, coins continued to develop.

After the American Revolution, the coining of money by private individuals or states was pro-hibited. The United States Mint at Philadelphia, which was then the capital of the United States, was the first building erected by Congress, and was the first public building to fly the flag. George Washington supplied some of his own silverware to run off a limited number of the first coins.

Coins of Early Colonial Times

(1) "Hog Money," about 1616, issued in the Sommer Islands (now Bermuda), was the first coinage issued for the early colonies.

(2) The New England Shilling, 1652, was issued from the first colonial mint near Boston, Massachusetts.

(3) The Pine Tree Shilling, 1667-74, was one of the coins issued to replace the easily counterfeited New England shillings, sixpence, and threepence.

(4) The Spanish Milled Dollar, struck in Mexico and known as a "piece of eight," was the most popular coin of the American colonies. It was accepted as legal tender in the United States until 1857.

(5) The Fugio Cent, 1787, the first coin ever issued by the United States as a nation, was privately struck under contract with the United States Government.

(6) The Bar Cent, 1785, with thirteen parallel bars representing the thirteen colonies, was one of many privately used coins issued before the establishment of an official United States mint.

(7) The Copper Cent, 1793, was one of the first coins issued by the United States Mint at Philadelphia when it went into full production.

(5)

(2)

BOSTO

NEW YORK
(6) CITY

PHILADELPHIA (3)

(7)

ATLANTIC
OCEAN

(4)

SOMMER ISLANDS
(BERMUDA)

(1)

MEXICO

This Spanish milled dollar was struck in Mexico. Obverse: Spanish coat-of-arms. Reverse: Mottoes entwined around the Pillar of Hercules. This may have been the origin of the dollar sign.

that they continued to be accepted as legal tender in the United States until 1857. This is the only foreign coin in United States history that has received this recognition.

The First Mint

As trade increased and the need for coins grew, the colonists decided to produce their own coins. In 1652, they established a

New England Shilling Issued in Massachusetts in 1652

mint in Massachusetts, at the outskirts of Boston. The first mint-master was John Hull, who continued to operate the mint despite the angry objections of King Charles II of England. The first coins of this mint were issued in shillings, sixpence, and threepence. However, these designs were so simple that they were easy to counterfeit. They were replaced by the famous Willow, Oak, and Pine Tree coins, which were minted until 1682.

Large Pine Tree Shilling, 1667-74

Oak Tree Threepence, 1660-67

Willow Tree Shilling, 1653-60

In order to issue these coins in opposition to the disapproval of King Charles II, all of the "tree" coins were dated 1652. Since the king had come to power in 1660, he was unable to prove that the coins were unauthorized issues.

Following the American Revolution and the Declaration of Independence in 1776, the Continental Congress authorized the issue of a new dollar. It was made of pewter, a metal composed mainly of tin, with small amounts of other metals added, such

Continental Dollar, 1776

as copper, zinc, or bismuth; there were also a few issues in brass and silver. The silver Continental dollar was the first American replacement for the Spanish milled dollar. However, it never reached general circulation. The obverse of the coin showed a sundial and the motto, "Mind Your Business." This legend, that is said to have been suggested by Benjamin Franklin, actually means that one should keep one's mind on one's work. The reverse contains the legend, "American Congress [encircled about] We Are One." This is surrounded by a circular chain with thirteen links. Each link contained a name of one of the original thirteen Colonies.

After the Articles of Confederation in 1778, the states had the right to issue their own coins. New Hampshire, Connecticut, Vermont, and New Jersey were the first states to do this; they arranged for their coins to be produced by private companies.

New Hampshire Halfpenny, 1776

Vermont Cent, 1787

Connecticut Cent, 1785

New Jersey Cent, 1786

Massachusetts established its own mint and issued copper cents and half-cents. The Massachusetts cent was valued at one one-hundredth of a Spanish dollar. This coin, struck in 1787 and

Massachusetts Copper Cent, 1787

1788, was the first official coin in the history of the world to be struck on a decimal basis. This system was favored by Thomas Jefferson, because it was easy to multiply and divide by ten. It has served as a model for most of the coins issued in the modern world.

The Fugio Cent

The first coin ever issued by the United States as a nation was the Fugio cent, in 1787. It is known today as the Franklin cent, because the design and the legends were supposed to have been originated by Benjamin Franklin. The coin was privately struck at mints in New Haven, Connecticut; New York City;

Fugio Cent, 1787

Rupert, Vermont, and in other places, under contract with the United States. Most of the copper for these coins came from the copper bands that held together the kegs of gunpowder sent to the Colonies by the French during the Revolutionary War. The word *fugio*, meaning "I fly," appears on the obverse. On the same side is a sundial and the legend, "Mind Your Business." On the reverse are thirteen circles linked together as a chain, and the words, "United States" and "We Are One."

The need for coins was growing at this period, but despite many discussions, a United States mint was not established. As a result, many private individuals issued coins or tokens for general circulation. Tokens were issued by private establishments as advertisements, and were not official coinage. Nevertheless, because they were often made of valuable metal, or were given a value, they circulated as coins. There was the Mott Token issued by tradesmen in New York, and the famous gold Brasher Doubloon issued in 1787. Only six of the latter are known, and these are so valuable that they are worth thousands of dollars to a collector—some say as high as $100,000. The well-known Bar Cent was issued in 1785. It bears no date and has thirteen parallel bars on one side to represent the original thirteen states.

The Mott Token was issued in 1789, as an advertisement, by William and John Mott, jewelry and watch dealers.

Brasher Doubloon, Issued by a Private Mint in 1787

The other side has the interlocking letters, USA. The design is said to have been copied from the buttons on the uniforms of Continental soldiers.

Bar Cent, 1785

A series of Washington coins or tokens circulated from 1783 to 1795. These bore the portrait of George Washington on the obverse and indicated a new feeling of patriotism among the young states. However, President Washington disliked the idea

Washington Piece, Issued in 1792, for Use as a Half Dollar

of anyone's portrait on a coin, including his own. It reminded him too much of the coins issued by countries ruled by monarchs. The United States shield and stars and the American Eagle that appeared on these coins later became standard on United States coins.

The United States Mint

The Founding Fathers recognized that if the new country was to prosper economically, it had to eliminate the widespread confusion caused by the great variety of coinage that was circulating throughout the states. Therefore, in writing the Constitution, the coining of money by private individuals or states was prohibited. Only one authority was to issue money—the federal government.

This ruling was considered so important to the new nation that a mint was established before any other federal institution. The United States Mint at Philadelphia, which was then the capital of the United States, was the first building erected by Congress and was the first public building to fly the flag. It was established by the Act of April 2, 1792, which also provided for the issuance of the following coins:

GOLD	VALUE
Eagle	$10.00
	(ten units or dollars)
Half Eagle	5.00
Quarter Eagle	2.50
SILVER	
Dollar	1.00
Half dollar	.50
Quarter dollar	.25
Disme (dime)	.10
Half disme	.05
COPPER	
Cent	.01
Half cent	.005

Since private coinage was now illegal, anyone who owned metal could bring it to the mint and have it made into money free of charge.

The new United States Mint was located on Seventh Street in Philadelphia. The first coins issued at the mint were the half disme and the disme. George Washington supplied some of his own silver plate to run off a limited number of these coins. The Liberty Head on the coins is believed to be modeled after Martha Washington.

Half Disme, 1792   Disme, 1792

One year later, in 1793, the Mint went into full production, coining copper cents and half cents. The supply of copper for these coins presented an immediate problem, and ads were placed in newspapers asking for copper to make coins. These ads attracted offers of utensils, nails, hardware from wrecked ships,

    Copper Half Cent, 1793

Copper Cent, 1793

and even included a teakettle and a pair of tongs donated by George Washington. The Mint was able to purchase sufficient copper to start production. In that year, the Mint produced 31,934 half cents valued at $159.67 and 112,212 large cents valued at $1,122.12. It must be remembered that production was slow in those days because machinery was simple and had to be worked by hand.

8

Official Copper Coins of the United States

Half Cent 1793-1857

THIS COPPER COIN and the large copper cent were the first official coins to be struck by the United States Mint. Half cents were the smallest denominations ever to be struck by the United States. Wages and prices were low in those days, and the half cent enabled individuals to purchase goods that cost less than one cent. Their chief use, however, was to make change for the Spanish silver *reales*. An eighth of a *real*, or a bit, was worth 12½ cents.

Half cents were not very popular with the public because they were not legal tender. That is, a bank, merchant, or individual did not have to accept them in payment of a debt. Four types of half cents were minted:

Liberty Cap, 1793-97   Draped Bust, 1800-08

Turban Head, 1809-35   Braided Hair, 1840-57

Large Cent 1793-1857

These coins are somewhat larger than the modern twenty-five-cent piece, and weigh exactly twice as much as the half cent. The dies for the chain or link type were produced in Paris by Jean Pierre Droz, a Swiss engraver. This coin was issued for one year only, 1793, because its design was subjected to a great deal of criticism by the public. Some claimed that Miss Liberty seemed

Chain or Link, 1793

to be frightened, and that the chains on the reverse implied that Liberty was in chains—a symbol not fit for a nation that had fought for and gained its freedom. As a result, a new engraver, Joseph Wright, was hired. He modified the design by replacing the chains with a laurel wreath. The large cent was struck each

Wreath, 1793   *Liberty Cap, 1793-96*

Draped Bust, 1796-1807   *Turban Head, 1808-14*

82

Coronet, 1816-39   *Braided Hair, 1839-57*

year from 1793 to 1857, with the exception of 1815. By 1857, the large coins became uneconomical to produce because the cost of copper, labor, and distribution to banks had risen. In addition, the coin was becoming unpopular because it was not legal tender.

Small Cent . . . . 1856 to Present

On February 21, 1857, Congress passed a new Coinage Act that halted the production of half cents and large cents. In addition, it decreed that foreign coins were no longer allowed to circulate and that all those having such coins could bring them to banks, where they would be exchanged for regular coins.

In 1856, the Flying Eagle cent made its appearance. It was made of an alloy consisting of 88 percent copper and 12 percent nickel. The addition of nickel gave these coins a whitish appearance. The nickel was added to discourage counterfeiting, since it made the alloy very hard and difficult to handle. Although it was a beautiful coin, it created problems, because the hardness of the metal made the detail in the eagle feathers difficult to reproduce. It was discontinued after 1858.

Flying Eagle, 1856-58

In 1859, the Indian Head cent, designed by James B. Longacre, was produced. Its obverse portrayed the head of an Indian girl wearing a headdress; the word LIBERTY appeared on the headband. It is believed that the head is actually that of Sarah Longacre, the designer's twelve-year old daughter. However, this idea is disputed, since close examination reveals that the features on the 1859 Indian cent resemble those on the 1849 gold dollar, which was designed before Longacre's daughter was born.

  Indian Head, 1859-1909

The Indian Head cent was made of 88 percent copper and 12 percent nickel. One year later, in 1860, the laurel wreath on the reverse was changed to an oak wreath, and a shield was added at the top. The composition of the metal remained the same from 1859 to 1864. Toward the end of the Civil War, in 1864, it was changed to a bronze alloy composed of 95 percent copper and 5 percent tin and zinc. The Indian Head cent was issued continuously until 1909, and is a favorite among coin collectors.

The Lincoln Head cent was first minted in the year 1909, to commemorate the 100th anniversary of the birth of Abraham Lincoln. These coins are the most popular among coin collectors because they are immediately available to start a collection. Even hard-to-find issues are relatively inexpensive, although certain coins cost one hundred dollars or more. The prices of scarce coins have continuously risen and will probably continue to rise in the future as the number of coin collectors increases.

The Lincoln cent was originally made of a bronze alloy consisting of 95 percent copper and 5 percent tin and zinc. This was the first of the coins in common circulation to carry a man's portrait, and it caused a great deal of excitement when issued. The coin came into existence when President Theodore Roosevelt decided to honor Lincoln's birthday. He commissioned Victor D.

Lincoln, 1909-58. Reverse: Wheat Stalks   *Lincoln, 1959 to Present. Reverse: Memorial*

Brenner to change the design on the Indian Head cent to that of a bust of Lincoln. The new penny was issued at the Philadelphia, Denver, and San Francisco mints. The engraver's initials, V.D.B., appeared on some 1909 and 1909-D issues. Protests arose because of the prominence of the initials on the coin, and these were removed. As a result, these coins are rare and quite valuable. The initials were replaced in 1918, on the obverse, below Lincoln's shoulder.

In the World War II year of 1943, the shortage of copper forced the United States Mint to use steel coated with zinc for the production of cents. A few 1943 cents made of copper are said to exist, although the mint does not acknowledge them as having been officially struck. It is possible that these were produced from bronze blanks that were accidentally left in the minting apparatus at the end of 1942. It should be emphasized, however, that many experts do not believe such coins exist.

In 1944, the Mint was able to obtain copper salvaged from shell cases, and it issued copper coins once more. In 1959, in celebration of the 150th anniversary of Lincoln's birthday, the wheat stalks on the reverse of the coin were replaced by a replica of the Lincoln Memorial in Washington, D.C. In 1962, the composition of the bronze was changed; the tin was removed and the new alloy was composed of 95 percent copper and 5 percent zinc.

Two-Cent Piece 1864-1873

This bronze coin was issued to relieve the tremendous demand for coins toward the end of the Civil War. The two-cent piece lasted only ten years because it lost its usefulness as soon as a sufficient number of one-cent pieces were struck. This coin

85

is of interest because it was the first United States coin to carry the motto, "In God We Trust," which now appears on all United States coins.

The request for an expression of religious sentiment upon our currency arose during the Civil War, when the Union Army suffered reverses at Fort Sumter, South Carolina, and at Bull Run, a small stream in Virginia, only thirty miles from Washington, D.C. One of the letters received by Salmon B. Chase, Secretary of the Treasury in Lincoln's cabinet, was from the Reverend M. R. Watkinson of Ridleyville, Pennsylvania. He wrote: "One fact touching our currency has hitherto been seriously overlooked. I mean the recognition of the Almighty God in some form on our coins. What if our Republic were now shattered beyond reconstruction? Would not the antiquaries of succeeding centuries rightly reason from our past coins that we were a heathen nation?" He suggested the motto, "God, Liberty, Law."

Secretary Chase wrote to the Director of the Mint in Philadelphia: "The trust of our people in God should be declared on

Two-Cent Piece, 1864-73

our national coins. You will cause a device to be prepared without unnecessary delay with a motto expressing in the fewest and tersest words possible, this national recognition."

In 1864, the two-cent piece appeared bearing the motto, "In God We Trust."

9

Official Silver and Nickel United States Coins

Three-Cent Piece . . . . 1851-73 (Silver)
1865-89 (Nickel)

THE SILVER THREE-CENT PIECE is the smallest and thinnest United States coin ever produced. One of the reasons that this coin was

Three-Cent Piece, Silver, 1851-73   *Three-Cent Piece, Nickel, 1865-89*

struck was to make it easy to purchase the then new three-cent stamps. In 1865, the silver coins were replaced by a larger three-cent piece made of nickel, copper, and zinc. The purpose of this coin was to redeem the three-cent paper notes issued during the Civil War. Thus, for a period of nine years, between 1865 and 1873, two coins, of different metals and design but of equal denomination, were being issued at the same time. After a while, the three-cent pieces lost their popularity, and they were discontinued in 1889.

Half-Dime 1794-1873

This silver coin was minted in several varieties, and was originally called the half disme. Until 1829, the half disme showed no indication of its value on either side. This omission caused some confusion when these coins were first issued, for other new coins were being issued at the same time. The half dimes were struck at Philadelphia, New Orleans, and San Francisco. In 1796, the word, "LIKERTY" appears instead of "LIBERTY," because of a broken die; these rare issues sell for several hundred dollars in Fine condition. In 1800, the word, "LIBEKTY," appears.

Liberty Flowing Hair, 1794-95

Draped Bust, 1796-1805

Liberty Cap, 1829-37　　　　*Liberty Seated, 1837-73*

Nickel Five-Cent Piece . . . . 1866 to Present

This very useful coin is struck from an alloy composed of 75 percent copper and 25 percent nickel. Its original purpose was to redeem the five-cent paper notes that had been issued during the Civil War. Eventually, it replaced the silver half dime and it has been one of our most useful coins. Four types of five-cent pieces have been issued since 1866. The Shield type, issued in 1866, has on the reverse the number "5" encircled by thirteen stars and thirteen rays; in 1867, the rays were eliminated. Among the rarest of all nickels are the 1877 and 1878 Shield type, for only a limited number of proofs were issued. The rarest of all nickels is the famous 1913 Liberty Head nickel. Five specimens are known to exist in private collections. These coins are unofficial and are believed to have been illegally struck.

When the Liberty Head nickel was issued in 1883, over five million were struck with the Roman numeral "V" on the reverse; the word, "CENTS," was omitted. As a result, some dishonest people gold-plated the coins and passed them off as new five-dollar gold pieces. Later that same year, the word, "CENTS," was added.

In 1913, the popular Indian Head or Buffalo type of nickel was issued. Two varieties were struck the first year. The first type shows the buffalo (really a bison) on a raised mound and the words, "FIVE CENTS," across the mound. Later, the mound was redesigned to form a thin, straight line, and the area below the line was flattened to prevent the letters, "FIVE CENTS," from protruding above the surface of the coin. The bison was modeled after Black Diamond, who was born and lived at the New York Zoological Gardens. The designer, James E. Fraser, employed three different Indians so as to form a composite of the Indian Head appearing on the obverse of the coin.

Our present five-cent piece, the Jefferson nickel, appeared in 1938. It was the first United States coin to picture an actual building rather than a symbol, such as an eagle or a stalk of wheat. The reverse shows Monticello, Thomas Jefferson's home near Charlottesville, Virginia. This coin was also the first United States coin for which a design was chosen in open competition. The winner, Felix Schlag, was awarded a prize of $1,000.

In 1942, the composition of the alloy was changed because nickel was a critical war material. From 1942 to 1945, the new five-cent piece was made of an alloy containing 56 percent copper, 35 per cent silver, and 9 percent manganese. To indicate that there was a change, the letter P was placed above the building on the reverse. This was the first time a P was ever shown on a coin struck at Philadelphia. In 1946, the use of the original nickel alloy was resumed, and the P mint mark was eliminated.

Shield, 1866-83   *Liberty Head, 1883-1912*

Buffalo or Indian Head, 1913-38   *Jefferson, 1938 to Present*

Dime . . . . 1796 to Present

This coin was first issued in 1796 and was originally known as the "disme." There are so many varieties and odd situations in the early issues that these coins have been a favorite among collectors, despite the fact that the dismes are rare and expensive. They have been minted at Philadelphia, New Orleans, Denver, San Francisco, and Carson City, Nevada.

One of the mysteries surrounding these dimes involves the 1871-CC issue. According to official mint records, 20,100 of these dimes were struck, yet the coin is so rare today that one of these dimes in Fine condition has sold for two hundred to three hundred dollars. The rarest of the dimes is the 1849-S. Only twenty

90

four were minted, and a specimen of this coin was sold in 1961 for $13,000!

Liberty Head, 1795-1807   *Liberty Cap, 1809-37*

Liberty Seated, 1837-91   *Liberty Head, Barber, 1892-1916*

In 1916, a new dime appeared. It was known as the Mercury Head dime, because the obverse looked like Mercury, the Roman god of commerce, who, according to legend, wore a winged helmet. Actually, the head is meant to represent Liberty, and the wings on her cap symbolize freedom of thought.

The Roosevelt dime appeared in 1946, the year after the death of the thirty-second President, Franklin Delano Roosevelt.

Winged Liberty, Mercury, 1916-45   *Roosevelt, 1946-65*
                                            Roosevelt, Clad, 1965 to Present

The issue was unusual, in that never before in United States history had a coin been issued so soon after the death of an individual. Most of these coins are easily available, with the exception of the 1949-S and 1955, 1955-D, and 1955-S. In those

R1658

years fewer coins were minted. The Roosevelt dimes will undoubtedly increase in value.

The composition of the dime was changed in 1965, but the new coin was not issued until 1966. It bore a 1965 date. On August 1 of that year the coins began to be issued with a 1966 date. All silver was eliminated, and the dimes were manufactured from strips composed of three layers of metal bonded together. The face of these "clad" coins is of 75 percent copper and 25 percent nickel. The insides are of pure copper, and can be seen at the edges of the coins.

Twenty-Cent Piece 1875-1878

This coin had the shortest life of any United States coin. It was so similar in design, size, and appearance to the quarter dollar, that many people were deceived and took this coin for a quarter. People soon refused to accept it from banks, and

Twenty-Cent Piece, 1875-78

it was officially discontinued in 1878. Actually, it was discontinued before that time, since in 1877 and 1878 only proofs were made. An interesting characteristic of this coin is that its edge is smooth instead of reeded. Ten thousand 1876-CC coins were struck but, except for a few coins, were melted by the mint. There are only fourteen of these coins known to exist, and one of these sold for $6,900 in 1961.

Quarter Dollar . . . . 1796 to Present

When this coin was issued in 1796, it showed no mark indicating its value. It was not issued again until 1804, and the value 25C was added to the reverse. During both of these years, these

Bust, 1796-1807

Liberty Cap, 1815-38

Liberty Seated, 1839-91

Liberty Head, Barber, 1892-1916

coins were issued in very small quantities. In 1796, only 5,894 pieces were issued; in 1804, 6,738 pieces were issued. In 1866, the motto, "IN GOD WE TRUST," was added to the reverse of the Seated Liberty issue. Many minor and major changes have appeared since the inception of these coins, and all of them are becoming of increasing interest to collectors.

Liberty Standing, 1916-30

The quarter that is in use at the present time is the Washington Head type. It was issued in the year 1932 to honor the 200th anniversary of George Washington's birthday. In 1965, the composition of the metal in the quarter was changed to the same that was to be used for the new clad dime. It is a sandwich, containing a center of pure copper. The face of the clad quarter is 75 percent copper and 25 percent nickel, which is the same as that used in the present five-cent piece.

Washington Head, 1932-65
Washington Head, Clad, 1965 to Present

Half Dollar . . . . 1794 to Present

The half dollar was first issued in 1794. It has been of great interest to collectors because of the many varieties and errors occurring in the production of this coin. Until 1836, the coins had the words, "FIFTY CENTS OR HALF A DOLLAR," lettered around the outer narrow edge. A year later, a new half dollar was

Bust, 1794-1807

Liberty Cap, 1807-39

94

Liberty Seated, 1839-91

Liberty Head, Barber, 1892-1915

Liberty Walking, 1916-47

Franklin-Liberty Bell, 1948-63

released with a reeded edge, and the value, "50 CENTS," appeared on the reverse.

The Franklin half dollar appeared in 1948, but lasted only sixteen years. Benjamin Franklin is the only person not a president to be honored on a regular coin. In 1964, the Kennedy half dollar was issued to honor our thirty-fifth president, John F. Kennedy. However, before this could be done, special legislation had to be enacted to allow the change, for, according to law, a design had to remain for at least twenty-five years. The obverse was designed by Gilroy Roberts, Chief Engraver of the United States Mint. The reverse shows the coat of arms of the President; it was designed by Frank Gasparro. Although almost four hundred million of these coins have been minted, the coin is rarely seen in circulation, because people believe it is a commemorative

Kennedy, 1964-65
Kennedy, Clad, 1965 to Present

issue to be distributed only once. However, the Mint will produce it for twenty-five years or more, as required by law.

A Kennedy half dollar of different composition was issued in 1966, but was dated 1965. However, starting August 1, 1966, all coins were produced with the 1966 date. This Kennedy half dollar is a clad coin like the new quarter and the dime. However, its two outer layers consist of 80 percent silver and 20 percent copper; its core is 21 percent silver and 79 percent copper. Its overall composition is 40 percent silver and 60 percent copper.

Dollar 1794-1935

The silver dollar was authorized by the Act of April 2, 1792, and was first issued in 1794. Until 1804, all silver dollars had the letters, "HUNDRED CENTS, ONE DOLLAR OR UNIT," inscribed around the outer narrow edge. There was a lapse in

*Bust,
1794-1804*

*Liberty Seated,
1840-73*

coinage until 1840, when these coins were issued with reeded edges.

The dollar is the basic unit of the United States decimal coinage system. The dollar is equivalent to one hundred units, and each coin less than a dollar can be described by an exact figure in the decimal system. Thus, a cent, or 1/100 of a dollar, is $.01; a nickel is $.05; a dime is $.10; a quarter is $.25; a half is $.50; and a dollar is $1.00. Any combination of coins can be easily and exactly expressed in this system: A quarter and two cents is $.27.

The name of the dollar comes from a large silver coin that was in use in the sixteenth century in Joachimsthal, in Bohemia. This coin was called the *Joachimsthaler*, which was later shortened to *taler*. The coin became so popular that many European countries adopted similar coins and gave them names derived

Liberty Head, Morgan, 1878-1921

from the taler. Our own "dollar" is derived from this German word. The Joachimsthaler is the ancestor of all silver dollar-size coins, including the Spanish piece of eight or milled dollar which directly influenced our own silver dollar.

An interesting silver dollar is the Trade dollar issued from 1873 to 1885, for use in China. After the Civil War, in order to compete with other countries for this trade, the United States Mint issued a special silver dollar. This dollar was designed to compete with the Mexican silver peso, which was the most popular coin in the Orient because of its silver content. The Trade dollar weighed more than our standard domestic silver dollar; its weight and purity—420 GRAINS . . . 900 FINE— appears on the reverse of the coin. The term 900 FINE means that 90 percent of the coin is silver (10 percent is copper). An interesting feature on many of these coins is that they have Chinese symbols or cuts made in them by Chinese merchants to

Trade, 1873-85

mark or check their silver content. Trade dollars are no longer legal tender in the United States and may not be used as a medium of exchange.

Another interesting coin is the Peace dollar issued in 1921, to celebrate the ending of World War I in 1918. This coin was

Peace, 1921-35

suggested by a convention of the American Numismatic Association in 1920. It was issued until 1935 and was the last silver dollar issued.

10

Collecting Gold Coins

GOLD IS THE MOST BEAUTIFUL and most durable of all metals. It is one of the few metals so chemically inactive that it will not change color or corrode upon prolonged exposure to air or to ordinary chemicals. Its use as an ornament in ancient times led to its use as a medium of exchange. Its value is so universally recognized that it serves as an international standard for monetary values. Although gold has not circulated as currency in the United States since 1933, our paper money is backed by the gold reserve stored in bullion form at Fort Knox, Kentucky, by the United States Treasury.

The first gold coins minted for the United States were the five-dollar half eagle and the ten-dollar eagle; they were struck in 1795. However, until the discovery of gold in California, in 1848, the metal was in short supply. After the discovery, gold became so plentiful that a gold dollar was authorized in 1849 and was issued for forty years. Another result of the gold rush was the issuance of the twenty-dollar double eagle. In 1849, only one double eagle was struck. That coin is now in the United States Mint collection at Philadelphia. One year later, 1,170,261 of these coins were minted. The following is a list of gold coins issued from 1795-1933:

Dollars

    Liberty Head, 1849-54

Small Indian Head,
1854-56

Large Indian Head,
1856-89

Quarter Eagle ($2.50)

Liberty Cap, No Stars,
1796

Liberty Cap, Stars,
1796-1807

Liberty Bust,
1808

Liberty Bust,
Reduced Size, 1821-34

Liberty Bust, Cap Replaced
by Ribbon, 1834-39

Liberty Coronet,
1840-1907

101

Indian Head, 1908-29

Three Dollars

Indian Head, 1854-89

Four Dollars

Flowing Hair, Barber,
1879-80 (430 Issued)

Coiled Hair, Morgan,
1879-80 (20 Issued)

Half Eagle ($5.00)

Liberty Cap, Facing Right,
1795-1807

Liberty Cap, Facing Left,
1807-34

Liberty Cap, Ribbon,
1834-38

Liberty Coronet,
1839-1908

Indian Head, 1908-29

Eagle ($10.00)

    *Liberty Cap, 1795-1804*

Liberty Coronet, 1838-1907

Indian Head, 1907-33

Double Eagle ($20.00)

Liberty Coronet, 1849 (Only One Struck); Liberty Coronet, 1850-1907

Liberty Standing, 1907-33 (1933 Coins Not Circulated)

11

Commemorative Coins

COMMEMORATIVE COINS are issued by nations to honor famous people, places, and events. In the United States, such coins must be authorized by special legislation, which is passed by the House of Representatives and the Senate, and signed by the President. Unlike coins issued for circulation, the Treasury Department does not handle distribution of commemorative issues. Instead, the United States Mint turns them over at face value to private agencies that have petitioned Congress to issue coins to commemorate certain historical occasions in which they have a particular interest. The private agency sells these coins above face value in order to raise money to celebrate and publicize these events, or to pay for monuments.

Commemorative coins are unique in that they are our most beautiful coins, and offer to the collector a fine cross section of American history. The first commemorative coin was the Columbian Exposition half dollar, issued in the year 1892, to honor the 400th anniversary of Christopher Columbus' voyage.

Columbian Exposition Half Dollar

Columbian Exposition Isabella Quarter

Most commemorative coins were issued as silver half dollars; there are forty-eight types. Only one coin, the Isabella, was issued as a quarter, in 1893; and only one coin, the Lafayette Memorial, was issued as a silver dollar, in 1900. Ten gold coins

Lafayette Monument Dollar

have been issued, ranging in face value from $1.00 to $50.00. No commemorative coins have been minted since 1954. The following is a list of United States commemorative coins that have been issued by the United States Mint from 1892-1954:

Commemorative Coin	Year	Denomination	Mint*
Columbian Exposition	1892, 1893	$0.50	P
Columbian Exposition (Isabella)	1893	.25	P
Lafayette Monument	1900	1.00 (silver)	P
Louisiana Purchase	1902, 1903	1.00 (gold)	P
Lewis and Clark Exposition	1904, 1905	1.00 (gold)	P
Panama Pacific Exposition (Octagonal)	1915	50.00 (gold)	S
Panama Pacific Exposition (Round)	1915	50.00 (gold)	S
Panama Pacific Exposition	1915	2.50 (gold)	S
Panama Pacific Exposition	1915	1.00 (gold)	S

Panama Pacific Exposition	1915	.50	S
McKinley Memorial	1916, 1917	1.00 (gold)	P
Illinois Centennial	1918	.50	P
Maine Centennnial	1920	.50	P
Landing of the Pilgrims	1920, 1921	.50	P
Alabama Centennial	1921	.50	P
Missouri Centennial	1921	.50	P
Grant Memorial	1922	1.00 (gold)	P
Grant Memorial	1922	.50	P
Monroe Doctrine Centennial	1923	.50	S
Huguenot-Walloon Tercentenary	1924	.50	P
Stone Mountain Memorial	1925	.50	P
Lexington and Concord	1925	.50	P
Fort Vancouver	1925	.50	S
California 75th Anniversary	1925	.50	S
Sesquicentennial of Declaration of Independence	1926	2.50 (gold)	P
Sesquicentennial of Declaration of Independence	1926	.50	P
Oregon Trail	1926	.50	P, S
Oregon Trail	1928	.50	P
Oregon Trail	1933, 1934	.50	D
Oregon Trail	1936	.50	P, S
Oregon Trail	1937	.50	D
Oregon Trail	1938, 1939	.50	D, P, S
Battle of Bennington	1927	.50	P
Hawaii	1928	.50	P
Daniel Boone Bicentennial	1934	.50	P
Daniel Boone Bicentennial	1935-1938	.50	D, P, S
Maryland Tercentenary	1934	.50	P
Arkansas Centennial	1935-1939	.50	D, P, S
Texas Centennial	1934	.50	P
Texas Centennial	1935-1938	.50	D, P, S
Spanish Trail (Cabenza de Vaca)	1935	.50	P
City of Hudson	1935	.50	P
San Diego Exposition	1935	.50	S
San Diego Exposition	1936	.50	D
Connecticut Tercentenary	1935	.50	P
Providence Tercentenary	1936	.50	D, P, S
Columbia Sesquicentennial	1936	.50	D, P, S
Cincinnati 50th Anniversary	1936	.50	D, P, S
Long Island Tercentenary	1936	.50	P
Cleveland Centennial	1936, 1937	.50	P

Bridgeport Centennial	1936	.50	P
Wisconsin Centennial	1936	.50	P
Lynchburg	1936	.50	P
Albany	1936	.50	P
Elgin Centennial	1936	.50	P
York County, Maine	1936	.50	P
San Francisco-Oakland Bay Bridge	1936	.50	S
Robinson (Arkansas)	1937	.50	P
Raleigh	1937	.50	P
New Rochelle	1937	.50	P
Swedes in Delaware	1937	.50	P
Gettysburg	1937	.50	P
Norfolk	1937	.50	P
Antietam	1937	.50	P
Iowa	1937	.50	P
Booker T. Washington	1946-1951	.50	D, P, S
Booker T. Washington-George Washington Carver	1951-1954	.50	D, P, S

*P = Philadelphia
 D = Denver
 S = San Francisco

Louisiana Purchase Jefferson Gold Dollar

Lewis and Clark Exposition Gold Dollar

*Panama-Pacific Exposition
Half Dollar*

108

Illinois Centennial Half Dollar

Landing of the Pilgrims Half Dollar

California 75th Anniversary Half Dollar

Sesquicentennial of Declaration of Independence Half Dollar

109

Iowa Centennial Half Dollar

*Booker T. Washington-
George Washington Carv-
er Half Dollar*

12

Where to Find Mint Marks

DUE TO ITS SMALL SIZE, it is sometimes difficult for the beginning collector to locate the mint mark. This is especially true when it shows signs of wear. The following is a list of mint marks and their locations on some of the most common coins:

Indian Head Cent—On the reverse, under the wreath; only the 1908 and 1909 cents have mint marks—the letter S.

Lincoln Cent—On the obverse, beneath the date.

Liberty Head Nickel—On the reverse, to the left of CENTS. The only mint marks are S and D, in 1912.

Buffalo Nickel—On the reverse, under FIVE CENTS.

Jefferson Nickel—On the reverse, to the right of the building; above the dome during the years 1942-1945.

Liberty Seated Dime—On the reverse, under or within the wreath.

Liberty Head Dime (before 1916)—On the reverse, under the wreath.

Mercury Head Dime—On the reverse, to the left of the fasces.

Roosevelt Dime—On the reverse, at the left of the bottom of the torch.

Liberty Seated Quarter—On the reverse, under the eagle.

Liberty Head Quarter—On the reverse, under the eagle.

Standing Liberty Quarter—On the obverse, above and to the left of the date.

Washington Quarter—On the reverse, under the eagle.

Half Dollar—1838, 1839—The O mint mark is on the obverse above the date; all other dates up to 1915, mint marks are on the reverse under the eagle; 1916, on the obverse; 1917, on obverse and reverse; after 1917, on reverse at lower left; Franklin type, on reverse, above bell; Kennedy type, on reverse to lower left of the eagle.

Liberty Seated Dollar—On the reverse, under the eagle.

Liberty Head Dollar—On the reverse, under the eagle.

Peace Dollar—On the reverse, at left above the eagle's tail feathers.

13

Key Coins

A COLLECTOR OF CENTS, nickels, dimes, quarters, and halves, finds that he can obtain many of these coins quite easily in ordinary circulation. However, there are some coins in these groups that are no longer in common circulation, but are relatively inexpensive to purchase. As a collector builds up his collection, he finds that certain coins are so scarce and so much in demand that their prices are quite high. For instance, a 1927-D Mercury Head dime in Extra Fine condition is valued at $35.00. A 1927 Mercury Head dime in the same condition is only $1.50. Experience has shown that these relatively rare coins that are needed to complete a collection have shown the most rapid increase in price. Here is a list of key, or "controller," coins which have increased the value of collections and which offer possibilities for continued increase in value.

Indian Head Cents			**Lincoln Cents**		
	GOOD	FINE		GOOD	FINE
1864 (L on ribbon)	$15.00	$60.00	1909-S (VDB)	$120.00	$175.00
1869	14.00	35.00	1909-S	20.00	30.00
1870	12.00	30.00	1910-S	2.50	4.50
1871	19.00	45.00	1911-S	6.00	10.00
1872	25.00	50.00	1912-S	4.00	7.00
1877	80.00	175.00	1913-S	3.00	5.00
1908-S	16.00	25.00	1914-D	50.00	75.00
1909-S	75.00	130.00	1914-S	3.50	6.00

1915-S	3.50	6.00
1922	20.00	50.00
1922-D	2.50	5.00
1923-S	1.00	3.00
1924-D	8.00	15.00
1926-S	2.00	5.00
1931-D	2.50	5.00
1931-S	25.00	40.00
1933-D	2.00	5.00

Indian Head (Buffalo) Nickels

(Variety 1—bison on a mound)
(Variety 2—base shows a straight line)

	GOOD	FINE
1913-D (Var. 1)	$1.00	$3.00
1913-S (Var. 1)	3.00	6.00
1913-D (Var. 2)	10.00	20.00
1913-S (Var. 2)	20.00	40.00
1914-D	9.00	20.00
1914-S	1.00	6.00
1915-S	4.00	10.00
1917-D	2.00	5.00
1917-S	2.00	5.00
1918-D	1.50	4.50
1918-S	1.50	4.50
1919-D	1.50	5.00
1919-S	1.50	6.00
1921-S	5.00	15.00
1924-D	1.00	3.00
1924-S	2.00	7.00
1925-D	2.00	12.00
1925-S	2.50	10.00
1926-D	1.00	2.50
1926-S	2.00	10.00
1927-S	2.50	7.00

Jefferson Nickels

	GOOD	FINE
1939-D	$2.00	$4.50
1939-S	.50	1.00
1942-D	.25	.50
1950-D	15.00	25.00

Mercury Head Dimes

	GOOD	FINE
1916-D	$75.00	$150.00
1919-D	1.00	3.50
1919-S	1.00	3.50
1921	6.00	20.00
1921-D	6.50	25.00
1925-D	1.00	2.50
1926-S	1.00	6.00
1927-D	1.00	4.00
1931-S	1.50	4.00
1931-D	1.75	5.00

Roosevelt Dimes

	GOOD	FINE
1949	$0.20	$0.30
1949-S	.30	.40
1950-S	.30	.40
1951-S	.30	.40
1952-S	.20	.30
1955	.25	.60
1955-D	.25	.50
1955-S	.25	.40

Quarter Dollars—Standing Liberty

(Variety 1)

	GOOD	FINE
1916	$175.00	$350.00
1917-D	2.00	3.50
1917-S	3.50	7.00

(Variety 2—Eagle is higher; different arrangement of stars.)

	GOOD	FINE
1917	$2.00	$4.50
1917-D	4.00	10.00
1917-S	4.00	10.00
1918	2.50	7.00
1918-D	4.00	9.00
1918-S over '17	200.00	450.00
1919-D	14.00	35.00
1919-S	25.00	40.00
1920-D	6.00	17.00
1921	15.00	30.00
1923-S	28.00	50.00
1924-S	4.00	9.00
1926-S	2.50	5.00
1927-S	5.00	12.00

Quarters—Washington Head

	GOOD	FINE
1932-D	$8.00	$20.00
1932-S	5.00	14.00
1936-D	3.00	8.00
1937-S	1.00	3.00

1955-D	1.00	2.00

Half Dollars—Walking Liberty

	GOOD	FINE
1916-S	$4.00	$15.00
1917-D (on obverse)	1.50	5.00
1917-D (on reverse)	1.25	4.00
1917-S (on obverse)	3.00	20.00
1919	2.00	7.00
1919-S	2.00	15.00
1919-D	2.00	7.00
1921	4.00	15.00
1921-D	4.00	15.00
1938-D	4.00	7.00

Half Dollars—Franklin

	GOOD	FINE
1948	$2.00	$3.00
1949	1.00	2.50
1953	2.75	4.00
1955	5.00	8.00

14

Coin Glossary

Alloy—A mixture of two or more metals.

Base Metal—An inexpensive metal; a metal other than gold, silver, or platinum.

Billon—Gold or silver alloyed with a large amount of a lesser metal, such as copper, tin, or zinc.

Bit—One eighth of a Spanish milled dollar; 12½ cents.

Blank—A piece of metal that is to be struck with a design.

Bust—The head and upper portion of the body.

Bullion—Metal in bulk form; bars of metal.

Clad coins—Coins that are composed of three layers of metal bonded together.

Clipped coin—A coin from which some of the metal has been illegally cut or shaved, usually around the edge.

Commemorative coin—A coin issued to honor a person, place, or historical event.

Corrugated edge—The edge of a coin stamped with vertical lines; a reeded edge.

Countermark—A mark stamped over an existing design, changing its value or making it current in another country.

Debasement—Lowering the purity of a metal by adding a cheaper metal.

Die—A metal stamp bearing a design. It is used to strike a coin.

Double struck—A blurred design on a coin, caused by striking the coin twice.

Electrum—A natural mixture of gold and silver.

Face—Obverse of a coin containing the principal design.

Face value—The value as stated on a coin.

Fasces—A bundle of wooden rods tied together with a thong, with an ax blade in the center.

Field—The blank background on a coin that is not occupied by the design.

Flan—The blank metal used to make a coin; planchet.

Hoard—A hidden stock of coins.

Incuse—A design sunk into a coin, as opposed to a raised design.

Inscription—All letters, words, or numbers appearing on a coin.

Key coin—A hard-to-get coin needed to complete a collection.

Legal tender—Money that must be accepted, by law, as payment in financial transactions.

Legend—Words appearing on the surface of a coin along the curved edge.

Lettered edge—Letters that appeared around the narrow, up-and-down edge of earlier coins. The purpose was to prevent clipping.

Milled edge—The thick rim around a coin that forms a raised border.

Mint mark—A small letter or symbol on a coin to indicate where it was struck.

Numismatics—The science or study of coins and currency of all kinds.

Obverse—The "head" side of a coin. It usually bears the date.

Overstrike—A new design that has been struck over an earlier one.

Patina—A tone or coloring found on some coins, caused by action of the air.

Pattern—A trial piece run off to test a proposed design or metal.

Planchet—The blank metal disk from which a coin is struck; also called a blank or flan.

Proof—A coin especially struck for collectors. It usually has a mirror-like finish; coins having a frosty surface are called matte proofs.

Reeded edge—Vertical markings around the edge of a coin to prevent clipping; also called corrugated or grained edge.

Relief—A design that is raised above the surface of a coin. The designs on a cent or a dime are in relief.

Restrike—A coin struck at a later date from original dies.

Reverse—The back or "tail" side of a coin.

Series—Coins of a single type such as the Roosevelt dime series.

Token—A piece struck by private individuals or companies in imitation of a coin, to be used for advertising or as a medium of exchange in transactions with that company.

15
Books About Coins

A.B.C.'s of Coin Investing, by E. P. Thomas *(Payne Publishing Company, 1965)*

America's Foreign Coins, by Oscar G. Schilke and Raphael E. Solomon *(Coin and Currency Institute, Inc., 1964)*

The American Journal of Numismatics, by American Numismatic Society

Ancient Coins: How to Collect for Fun and Profit, by Ted G. Wear *(Doubleday and Co., 1965)*

Ancient Greek and Roman Coins, by G. F. Hill *(Argonaut, Inc., 1964)*

Ancient Numismatics, by Kurt Regling *(Argonaut, Inc., 1965)*

Appraising and Selling Your Coins, by Robert Friedberg *(Sterling Publishing Company, 1966)*

A Catalogue of the World's Most Popular Coins, by Fred Reinfeld *(Sterling Publishing Company, 1956)*

Coin Collecting, by Fred Reinfeld & Robert V. Masters *(Sterling Publishing Company, 1966)*

Coin Collecting for Fun and Profit, by Editors of Coin World *(Arco Publishing Company, 1964)*

Coin Collectors Handbook, by Fred Reinfeld *(Doubleday and Co., 1966)*

Coin Investors Manual, by Editors of Coin Dealer Newsletter *(Payne Publishing Company, 1965)*

COINS, by John Porteaus *(G. P. Putnam and Sons, 1964)*

COINS HAVE TALES TO TELL, by Frances W. Browin *(J. B. Lippincott Company, 1966)*

COINS OF THE WORLD, by R. A. G. Carson *(Harper and Bros., 1962)*

COLLECTORS GUIDE BOOK TO COINS, by Hans Holzer *(Simon and Schuster, 1965)*

THE COMPLETE BOOK OF COIN COLLECTING, by Joseph Coffin *(Coward-McCann, 1959)*

FACTS AND FICTIONS ABOUT COINS, by Leon Lindheim *(World Publishing Company, 1966)*

FELL'S INTERNATIONAL COIN BOOK, by Jacques Del Monte *(Frederick Fells, Inc., 1960)*

GOLD COINS OF THE WORLD, by Robert Friedberg *(Sterling Publishing Company, 1965)*

A GUIDE BOOK OF UNITED STATES COINS, by R. S. Yeoman *(Whitman Publishing Company, 1967)*

THE GUIDE TO NORTH AMERICAN COINS, by Arthur Liebers *(Arco Publishing Company, 1961)*

NUMISMATICS—AN ANCIENT SCIENCE, by Elvira Eliza Clain-Stefanelli *(Superintendent of Documents, Government Printing Office, 1965)*

UNITED STATES COINS, by Arthur Liebers *(G. P. Putnam and Sons, 1965)*

UNITED STATES COMMEMORATIVE COINAGE, by Arlie R. Slabaugh *(Whitman Publishing Company, 1963)*

16

Photo Index of Coins and Odd Money

Ancient Coins and Media of Exchange

Odd Money

Early American Coins

Official Coins of the United States

17

Index

About the Book

Denarius, drachma, louis d'or, doubloon, shilling, dime—to some these coins represent merely a medium of exchange, but to the coin collector they evoke visions of strange foreign lands and customs, stimulating an interest not only in monetary values but in the geography, history, and even languages of the rest of the world.

An introduction to the exciting and educational hobby of coin collecting, this book tells the fascinating story of coinage, from the beginnings of barter through the development of ancient Greek and Roman civilizations.

A section dealing with the techniques of coin collecting—how to store coins, where to find coins of value, and what kinds of coins to collect—should be of inestimable value to the budding numismatist. Another section, devoted to United States coins, includes a photo story of coin production at the United States Mint and a list of all our commemorative coins.

Profuse illustrations and photographs enable both the beginner and the advanced collector to identify coins and to learn about their place in history.

Although addressed to the young reader, THE STORY OF COINS will prove highly useful to anyone seeking an easy-to-read yet authoritative guide to the popular hobby of coin collecting.